Cracked

of related interest

Living with Brain Injury
Philip L. Fairclough
ISBN 1 84310 059 2

My Brain Tumour Adventures
The Story of a Little Boy Coping with a Brain Tumour
Sharon Dempsey
Illustrated by Gabbie Collins
ISBN 1 84310 125 4

The Pits and the Pendulum
A Life with Bipolar Disorder
Brian Adams
ISBN 1 84310 104 1

Cracked

Recovering After Traumatic Brain Injury

Lynsey Calderwood

Foreword by Dr Robert McCabe

Jessica Kingsley Publishers
London and Philadelphia

First published in the United Kingdom in 2003
by Jessica Kingsley Publishers Ltd
116 Pentonville Road
London N1 9JB, England
and
325 Chestnut Street
Philadelphia, PA 19106, USA

www.jkp.com

Library of Congress Cataloging in Publication Data
Calderwood, Lynsey, 1978-
   Cracked : recovering after traumatic brain injury / Lynsey Calderwood.
   P.cm.
   Included bibliographical references.
   ISBN 1-84310-065-7 (pbk. : Alk. Paper)
   1. Calderwood, Lynsey, 1978---Health. 2. Brain
damage--Patients--Rehabilitation--Great Britain--Biography. 3. Brain--Wounds and injuries--Complications--Patients--Great Britain--Biography. I. Title.

RC387.5 .C35 2002
617.4'810443'092--dc21
[B]
                                                        2002016246
A CIP catalog record for this book is available from the Library of Congress

British Library Cataloguing in Publication Data
A CIP catalogue record for this book is available from the British Library

ISBN 1 84310 065 7

Printed and Bound in Great Britain by
Athenaeum Press, Gateshead, Tyne and Wear

Contents

For all those who have ever suffered a brain injury;
their families and their carers.

Foreword

You'd only hit your head when you fell off the chair for goodness sake...it wasn't as if you'd fallen twenty feet. The doctors in the hospital you'd stayed in overnight said you'd be as right as rain in a few days. Of course, here in the west of Scotland it rains cats and dogs!

But now you didn't just get back into your old ways... No in fact things went really odd – you could no longer play your favourite computer games so easily, any longer. Almost as if that night you were in the hospital bed some electronics-mad gremlin came and messed up the programme without telling you. Oh, and what about the business of not being able to recognize your old primary school friends any longer? And the work you could do before almost with your eyes closed at school was suddenly really difficult.

Imagine it, if you can.

Well, you probably wouldn't get close to imagining how dreadful it could be to find your brain has suddenly messed up big style after a head injury. This revealing story tells what happened to one not so ordinary Renfrew adolescent in November 1992. Lynsey is that not quite so ordinary individual. She has had her life turned upside down and slowly, painfully has managed to get herself right side up again for the most part. She displayed resilience and emotional courage to persevere when nothing proved easy: the personal struggle of coping with an extended stay in an adolescent psychiatric unit – an all too stark reminder of the virtual absence of specialist rehabilitation settings for young people who sustain severe head injuries; the daunting struggle of returning to her former mainstream secondary school only minimally equipped to provide the levels of extra support required; the distressing realization that friendships exposed to such difficulties rarely last; the awkwardness of changed relationships in a fragile and stressed family environment, where the others adjusted their ways to cope with the 'new' Lynsey.

Many adolescents facing such adversity would have crumbled into despair and hopelessness. That Lynsey did not was amazing. Her determination kept her slogging away, at times close to feeling overwhelmed but on she went. As the psychiatrist involved in her continuing mental health care I marvelled at her progress. Interestingly as she began to rebuild her shattered adolescent identity a new strand of creative energy emerged…Lynsey the poet, Lynsey the author.

This is her story. The account of a reconstructed identity. Read it and experience the regrowth of an adolescent spirit.

Roughly one million individuals of all ages sustain a head injury requiring attendance at A & E Departments at hospitals in the UK each year. Head injury affecting children and young people is sadly not an uncommon problem. Here are a few disconcerting facts:

- 2 per cent of all children will experience a head injury requiring hospital attendance

- 45,000 children under the age of sixteen sustain a head injury each year

- boys with head injury tend to outnumber girls two to one

- 300 children injured each year in this way die from their injuries.

Dr Robert McCabe, Consultant Adolescent Psychiatrist,
Gartnavel Royal Hospital

Chapter 1

How I Felt in the Beginning

'Who are you?' said the Caterpillar.
This was not an encouraging opening for a conversation.
Alice replied, rather shyly, 'I–I hardly know, sir, just at present – at
least I know who I was when I got up this morning, but I think I
must have been changed several times since then.'

Alice's Adventures in Wonderland, Chapter 5

I didn't even recognize my own face in the mirror. Nothing felt right. Dazed. Paralyzed by fear, my first instinct was to run but I had nowhere to hide. Pain exploded like fireworks behind my eyeballs and there was a sizzling in my skull like a chain saw. I tried to speak but I had a knot in my throat and my tongue felt thick and woolly. I was terrified I was going to choke. Voices echoed, ricocheting across the room. I wished they sounded familiar.

I felt like an infant. Of course, I didn't fully comprehend how this brain injury had changed me; I only sensed that my life would never be the same. I remember crying, feeling alone and being defenceless, but only for a day. I recall an anonymous nurse who held my hand in comfort while I begged so frantically for my memories. This part of me was dead, yet I was fighting to resuscitate it.

I remember feeling totally anonymous. I didn't fully comprehend what had happened to me. I remember crying, feeling isolated. I was no longer the child my mother gave birth to. I did not feel like HER. I was HER reflection but I felt too ambiguous to be a real flesh and blood person. However, on the outside I still looked like their daughter. I still looked like a normal average teenager. There were no bruises or fractures, no bandages around my head and no magic wand to reveal my imperfections.

When they dressed me up in HER clothes and showed me HER photograph, I thought she looked just like me too. That's when I began to feel threatened. Her shadow was beginning to haunt me and my family was trying to reincarnate her through me. I felt belittled by this overwhelming, overbearing ghost and everything that held a candle to her. It was as if I'd stepped through a mirror and here I was: the evil twin.

I'd been cheated. Cheated of my childhood. It was HER. It was all HER fault. SHE was the one. I blamed HER for my lack of memories. I HATED HER.

☙

My glassy stare penetrated the mirror as I glared defiantly at the girl who wasn't me. I studied the intricate indents of her inanimate face: vacant blue eyes, red-ringed and swollen; pink-red lips, drawn together in a childish pout; even the little dash mark scar I had acquired as a child – where I fell through the glass coffee table – didn't belong to me. The series of curves joined in the middle to form a nose wasn't mine either.

I sniffed. The nose twitched and I jumped back like a startled rabbit. The me that wasn't really me followed suit, so we began a game of copycat: I raised my eyebrows, so did she; I raised my hand, so did she. Going faster, I tried to trick her into making a mistake; finally, I lashed out, tried to punch her in the stomach.

AAAH

She blocked me. That hurt. I stared hard at her but I couldn't break her gaze. Her eyes were wild and angry; she looked like she hated me almost as much as I hated her.

I didn't want to be here. All I wanted to do was go home but, somehow, I'd stepped through the mirror and we'd switched places. I was trapped in a land of reflections.

❧

Fourteen years of stuff and nonsense, an autopsy of Lynsey's life. I wrestle with my mind because it feels like it is no longer attached to me. I feel like I've been shoehorned into an alien body. I shuffle through old papers and photos in random order like some private investigator. My memories have no structure. They are completely dislocated.

I'm actually breaking into a sweat, fighting my lazy, sedentary brain. One of the few things I have learned is that I lack hindsight. I have no understanding of past events. I'm trying to organize all HER junk. I keep looking at the photographs and then the days melt together and then I forget and do it all over again.

❧

I keep looking at the photographs and then the days melt together and then I forget and do it all over again. ☐

❧

I look at the pin-ups on the walls, the soft toys and the bedcovers I did not choose. I feel bitter when other people try to impose HER memories on me. I want to put it into words but there are no words to express clearly how I feel.

I have to remember the name of her sister when she comes back into the room.

But I never could remember. I wore my new identity like a child playing 'dress up'. Later, when I learned and explored my limitations, I could only ache for what I should have been. I was completely afraid of life, other children, myself. I couldn't understand just how much I had changed, how much my whole world (especially my body) didn't belong to me: I don't even know my own face. I don't even know my own body.

Maybe if I lose some fat, I'll find myself within the flesh. I wonder what I really look like? Being the second Lynsey means I already feel like I'm second best.

I want to be invisible.

I want to disintegrate into a pile of dust.

I just want to disappear.

ಸ

They say I look like my father. Her father. The father is lean with a thick crop of startling raven black hair. He looks younger than his forty years. The mother is short and plump, she has a kind face and soft pink cheeks. The sister is a cute button nosed ten-year-old with flaxen blonde hair and a peaches and cream complexion.

They are all strangers.

Most children go through a phase of gradual disenchantment whereas I had adolescence thrust upon me. My life seems so short and my memories so infantile that I feel like I know nothing whatsoever. As far as I'm concerned I was born in November 1992 (the day of my accident) and whatever happened in the world before that is a mystery.

> *'I wonder if I've been changed in the night? Let me think: was I the same when I got up this morning? I almost think I can remember feeling a little different. But if I'm not the same, the next question is, who in the world am I?'*

> *Alice's Adventures in Wonderland, Chapter 2*

Sometimes at night I would retreat to my room, look at my school photographs and read poems I had written. But instead of feeling closer to my past, I felt encumbered by the details of someone else's life.

> *'I'm sure I'm not Ada,' she said, 'for her hair goes in such long ringlets, and mine doesn't go in ringlets at all; and I'm sure I can't be Mabel, for I know all sorts of things, and she, oh! she knows such a very little! Besides, she's she, and I'm I.'*

> *Alice's Adventures in Wonderland, Chapter 2*

I keep a stash of memories on the tip of my tongue, in case I am in strange company that requires me to talk about my childhood and I don't want to explain myself: my invisible friends were called Christopher and Treebarcha; I had an eye operation when I was seven; children at school used to call me 'Barbara Taylor Bradford' on account of the pages of stories I used to write.

One of my favourite 'memories' is a story told to me by my younger sister, Nikki. She says that when we were younger I was the well-behaved child and she was the naughty one. She never misses an opportunity to tell me about the time when I poured a bowl of cornflakes over my own head. She had been annoying me, and I wanted to get her back. I was believed and Nikki was sent to her room but I think, in retrospect, I would have preferred her punishment to feeling my mother's fingers raking through my hair as she washed out all the soggy cornflakes.

My life was complicated: at fourteen years old I became public property. Everyone thought they were entitled to know who I was because of my disability. I hated this most of all. No one has the right to divulge my life history without my consent. But I didn't really have a choice. I was like some curious glass artefact. Everyone was afraid to handle me in case I broke; they didn't even know what was wrong with me. I'd look at myself in the mirror, and wonder who I was staring at.

It can't possibly be me. I wish I would just wake up…and pretend that nothing ever happened…and that all of this, was just a nightmare…

But I couldn't seem to wake up.

The inside of my skull vibrated like jelly. Words came to me slowly and fuzzily. I kept forgetting the names of things, and I constantly described objects that I had forgotten the names for. I used more difficult words to name simple things. Long, elaborate and complicated words were easier to remember. I became very frustrated, often shaking my head and saying 'I don't know'. My memory loss embarrassed me. I didn't like the way people looked at me as I stumbled over the words to describe a bike or a car.

'Ok. Take your time. Just one more test,' said the psychologist woman. She placed a blank piece of paper and took the little picture cards away. 'Can you draw the bike for me?' I sat squinting, trying to remember the simple image. Trying to remember what a bike looked like

…mmm…wheels, I know it has wheels…and handlebars…

I draw two round circles for wheels then collapse in tears, as I can't remember the rest. 'Ok. That's fine. That's enough,' she soothed. Abysmally, I had failed yet again.

❧

All my life, I've sought recognition and understanding. Ever hungry for admiration, all I've ever wanted is for people to like me. My insecurity and insatiable appetite for praise sprang from the ambition to live up to the memory of *the other Lynsey.* She died seven years ago, on exactly the same day as I was born. Everyone adored the other Lynsey. At first I longed to be just like her. I tried to adopt her personality, her likes and dislikes. I just wanted everyone to accept me. My family would tell countless stories about their other daughter, how wonderful she was, how flawless.

❧

I was going to be called Lynn, Lynda or Lynsey. 'Eventually,' said my mum, 'we just picked your name out of a hat!' Lynsay, Lyndsay, Lindsay, Linsay, Linsey and Linzi – these are just a few of the befuddled variations that I've been graced with over the years. Even my closest friends fail to spell my name correctly on birthday and Christmas cards. The one I really, especially, hate being called, though, is 'Lesley'.

At school, I hated sharing my name with two other girls and I resigned myself to being called by my surname: Calderwood. Of course, to complicate matters further, our class had two Donnas and three Garys.

After three years of living at 74c High Street, I became quite used to misspellings and mistaken identities but nothing had prepared me for the day when I received a letter addressed to: Mr Wendy Auldwood, 74 Sea-High Street.

15

Chapter 2

The Behavioural Unit

I don't remember the first hospital at all. My brain was all twisted like a pretzel. They said I was in the Neurosciences Department for a while but they couldn't find anything wrong. I just remember waking up one day and people asking me all these questions within questions:

walk   a   straight   line,
    touch   yourfinger to yournose.   What
happened? Do   you   re   member?

And the best one of all: Who's the prime minister?

God, they always ask me that. I wish they'd stop asking me that.

My concentration

    level is about fifteen minutes long,
    makes it hard to listen to what people are telling me

especially when there's more than one person talking
losing my

    balance and stumbling into furniture and other
    objects and walking into door frames. I couldn't
    properly judge distances anymore. None of my friends
    come

to visit me. I sometimes hear my mum and dad whispering about
how cruel they think my friends are.

I have also been having   blanking   out   spells
which come on with no warning. I can be talking to someone and I
just kind of   fre   eze.
They have to get my attention to bring me back.

❧

I don't know what happened. One minute, I was lying back, lapping
up the warmth of the hot bubble bath, gazing up at the ceiling when,
suddenly, the blue and green fishes on the mosaic tiles were

swimming across to meet me ～～～～～～～

～～～～～～～～～～～～～～～～～～～～～～～～

Suddenly, the water is freezing. I am flapping around while my dad is trying to scoop me out of the water. I look at him, indignantly.

How dare he barge in when I am taking a bath – And he's taken the door right off its hinges!

ॐ

Every Monday morning, the taxi rolls up outside our building and I am whisked off to a wonderful whimsical world where I play cards and make clay models under the watchful eye of the super psychiatric nurses:

I hate this place. Some kind of hospital. 'Cept it's not a hospital 'cause there's no beds.

I'm stuck here with all the problem-page cases under the sun: a schizophrenic, a school phobic, a manic-depressive, two hyper kids and a god-knows-what-else. Folk come and go and sometimes they come back and sometimes they don't. The ones that run this place – the nurses or whatever they are – they don't like me. They look at me like I'm a few bells short of a symphony.

What's a symphony? I think I just made that up

Today, we played instruments. Well, they did. But I didn't. They said I was 'antishoshal-'. Not interested anyway. The two hyper kids went mental with the big drumsticks, going round tapping everyone on the head. THEY weren't happy so the kids got put in the quiet room.

My jigsaw days spent at the behavioural unit feel empty and unexplored. My childlike curiosity is insatiable but patronizing staff refuse to accept my memory lapses and my vagueness. Apparently I am 'psychotic', 'bizarre' and 'paranoid'.

My appointed key worker is Agnes: a vertically, horizontally and diagonally challenged specimen, in her early forties.

Some folk call her Senga, I don't know why? It's mad. The folk in here are barking, some of them.

'Barking', that's what someone said to me, 'You've got to be barking to be in there.'

Angus! That's another name she gets called. I nearly thought she was a man first. She isn't even a doctor, I don't think.

The dyed poodle perm and pencilled-in eyebrows confirm for me that Agnes is, in fact, female and of human species. And it's my expert opinion that this Specimen suffers from an acute case of pizza-face-itis and her efforts to combat this with putrid orange foundation have resulted in what's commonly known as a 'tango-spam' syndrome. My colleagues, who have worked with the creature for quite some time, have also discovered that this affliction intensifies the auburn streaks that are rampaging through her woolly mop. Her inch-thick belt-skirts accentuate her already larger-than-life bottom.

On a home visit, she tells the parents I am 'a few shillings short of a pound!'

Furthermore, her behaviour is extremely bizarre: she believes we are her patients and in an effort to distract us from her obvious psychotic tendencies, she attempts to manipulate staff by use of clever mind games. It is in my expert opinion that the specimen lacks sufficient ability to control paranoid aggression and should be subject to having her face re-built by our junior plastic surgeons, the hyper-kid doctors.

There's only me and the nurses and a strange boy in this morning. I've never seen him before. He's pale and skeletal with black pointy eyebrows. His grey papery lips are cracked and hard and his eyes are like little pinholes.

'Like a match with the wood scraped off,' that's what my mum would say. I think he looks like a burnt match.

He asks me to play 'Guess Who' with him. I play because there's nothing else to do and because the nurses will call me 'anti-social' if I don't.

I might even make a friend.

'Right,' says Matchstick, 'Your turn to guess who.'
  'I don't know,' I say, looking around bewildered.
  'You must know,' he laughed, 'there's only one guy left.'
  I say the first name that comes into my head. 'Uh, Susan?'
  'No, it's a man – ' he pulls my board away from me – 'you were supposed to put all the women down. And that's not Susan.'
  'Oh.'
  'Right, I win. Play again,' he said, without looking up. He takes a yellow peg from the box and when I try to copy him he looks at me quizzically and says, 'What are you doing? You didn't win. You can't get one unless you win.'
  I slam my hand down hard on the table, 'I don't want to play anymore.'
  'You're batty,' he smirked, pointing a finger at his head and making circular motions.

> *'Do cats eat bats?'*
> *'Do cats eat bats?'*
> *and sometimes,*
> *'Do bats eat cats?'*
> *for you see, as she couldn't answer either question it didn't matter*
> *which way she put it.*

Alice's Adventures in Wonderland, Chapter 1

I've got a funny thing on my hand. It's like a little goofy tooth, sticking out of a mouth that my finger and thumb makes when I press them together, a bit like making a shadow puppet. I don't know where it came from. I don't think it was there yesterday. I'm busy investigating its big yellow volcano top when Matchstick says, 'Eugh warty, it's only frogs that get warts.'

'Don't pick that,' chastises the mother, 'It'll bleed and you'll end up with warts all over your hands.'

Well, I don't want it on my hand, anymore.

'Lynsey!' she shouts, in disgust, 'Don't bite that!'

There isn't even any blood. I thought there might be green or yellow blood but there's not even red blood. Why do I even need a plaster?

Dr Doom is the resident psychiatrist. She has a bowl hair cut and looks like a real-life Frankenstein's monster on hormone replacement therapy. She looks like she's been glued into her high-backed black leather swivel chair. I feel like I'm on trial and she is the judge, jury and executioner, all rolled into one. She doesn't even look up when I walk in; she simply continues to scribble cabalistic symbols in a fat black book.

Her office is plastered from floor to ceiling with shit yellow woodchip. There is a rumpled poster of a banana with a zip on it on one wall and a food chart on the other. A large clear jar of chocolates, with each individual chocolate wrapped in a different coloured sparkly-paper jacket, squats nervously on the edge of her black ash desk. Hiding behind her on the floor there is a scraggy wicker basket swamped with notelets and pamphlets and a sandwich pack that didn't come from the same trolley as the patients' mouldy lunches.

She keeps asking me stupid questions about school and my family: 'Where do you live?'

'Umm…'

'Hurry up, you must know where you live – What school do you go to?'

'Uh, umm…don't know,' I stammer.

'Who is the prime minister?'

Oh no, there's that question again. I don't have a clue.

No answer.

'You are a rude and arrogant young person. Very anti-social…' Blah, blah, blah… I sit there grinning like a Cheshire cat while she scribbles in her notebook. I don't know whether to cry or shout or laugh right in her face.

'Arrogant' and 'anti-social', that's what she called me.

Ar-o-gan-tuh…an-ti-sho-shal…arrogant…anti-social…
Arrogantantisocialarrogantantisocial

ARROGANTANTISOCIAL

ARROGANTANTISOCIAL!!!

I screamed at the top of my lungs, eyes wild with frustration, 'Mum, whassat mean?'

My mum's hand trembled, spilling tea onto the saucer. 'Sit down nicely, Lynsey.'

'Nonono*NO!*' I shrieked, tearing at my hair and coiling it around my index finger.

The Specimen asks me what I'd like to eat for lunch.

What do I like to eat?

She doesn't even wait for an answer, just rolls her eyes and then throws a plastic packaged sandwich at me like she's throwing scraps to a dog.

Maybe I should sit under the table?

There are two other girls in the lunchroom. One is fourteen but looks about twenty, she is tall and broad with lumpy putty-coloured skin and glazed eyes. Someone said, 'She looks like Lurch from the Addams family.' Sometimes she shares a taxi with me and she says people tell her she should be a model.

A model what? I like making models from Lego bricks and from clay.

Sometimes the Putty-model is friendly and talks continually and sometimes she doesn't even know who I am. She is something called a 'schizophrenic'. The other girl has short blonde hair and a perpetual smile. She's chatty and she giggles incessantly. She has something called a social phobia. Blondie tells me a story about how she used to sneak back into the house and hide in her wardrobe when her mum went out to work, instead of going to school.

I can't wait to start going to school. I'll go to school in her place.

The other day they gave me a weird salad sandwich. It was weird because it had a thing in it. I was eating it and eating it and trying to swallow all the leaves and grass and stuff and then

KER-RUNCH

OH!

I flipped open the lid of the sandwich. It was a circle-sandwich with big brown jaws just like a Pac-man on the computer. Leafing through the dry green mulch, I overturned a grisly tomato, only to find a hard pearly-white stone with a hole in its pink-tinged top. I turned it over on my hand for a moment before standing it up on its haunches on the table top and continuing to tackle the circle-sandwich.

OH!

I'd only taken another bite when I realized that the previously bland bread tasted very salty; it was wet and warm and soggy and it seemed to be changing colour at the corners.

Yuck! Don't want it any more.

I sat staring, giving it the evil eye; I was watching to see if it would mutate on the plate.

'Why aren't you eating? Hurry up?' The Specimen's eyes trailed between the mutant sandwich and me. 'What's this?' she said, picking up the pearly-stone between her thumb and her index finger. 'It wash ing the sangweesh,' I burbled between gulping a mouthful of blood. Little red rivulets were trickling from the corners of my mouth. 'Uurgh, disgusting,' she shrieked, 'Go to the toilet and get a tissue to stop the bleeding.'

I wanted to keep the pearly-white tooth. I thought it looked like a little pointy bit of marble. However, when I returned, it had been buried in the bin along with the corpse of the mutant circular sandwich.

For years, I had nightmares that my teeth were falling out. I'd wake up every morning, convinced I was toothless. The strangest dream I ever had was when all my teeth fell out, one by one, then turned into giant chess pieces as they hit the ground, which turned out to be a black and white chequered chess board.

In the afternoons we have art and crafts. The specimen gives me a massive sheet of orange sugar-paper and asks me to draw a picture. Ham-fisted, I clutch the chubby black crayon when she's not looking. Ruth (Blondie) is drawing a cottage in the country, she is using thin calm-coloured crayons and her work looks almost photographic.

She should be an artist.

I try to draw a picture just like Ruth. Start at the bottom left hand corner and work my way up.

RUTH

Ruth

'Why are you writing Ruth's name?'

I look at my own frenzied scribbles then tear the paper up in a rage.

They're all spying on me.

Even the mother and father are spying on me. The mother tries to trick me with a pen from Blackpool. I know it's from Blackpool because she took us to Blackpool for the day and that's where she got it and it has a moving picture of the Blackpool tower.

'Lynsey, what does that pen say?' she says.

'Blackpool.' I nearly say 'Blackpool tower' but I stop short, just in case it just says 'Blackpool' and nothing else.

If she says, 'What else does it say?' then I can always say 'tower'.

She doesn't say anything, though, so I know I got it right.

The classroom in the day centre is patrolled by a prune faced semi-geriatric with a complexion like a Spitting Image puppet and hair like wire wool; she wears brown ski-pants and polka dot blouses with big green and gold brooches.

Ruth and the Putty-model are only at the unit part-time, as they are slotting back into mainstream school; the hyper kids are usually running riot so Prune-face has to spend most of her time squawking at them; that leaves me and Matchstick unattended to whatever we want or don't want to do.

'Are you a virgin?' he casually drops into the conversation, one day.

'Eh?'

'Have you ever been shagged?' he says, leering at me.

'Shut up,' I fold my arms defensively.

'It's ok. I'm not a virgin either,' he says, 'I done it, last summer.' He is fourteen, exactly a month older than me, and exactly what he is supposed to have done last summer is a complete mystery.

He wants me to ask him all about his summer holiday but I won't because then he'll ask me what I did last summer and I can't remember.

Then Domino-girl is recruited into the classroom. She is a truant: the nurse-type-people all assume she doesn't want to go to school, they label her difficult and anti-social and then bracket her with the rest of us 'nutcases'. Truth is, all she wants is to move schools to be with her friends as she lives outside their catchment area.

If the nurses had asked Domino what she wanted, they might have found out sooner than six weeks into her stay. But they never asked us what we wanted, they just waffled their textbook semi-diagnosis and tried to stencil us as varying degrees of nutcase-ness.

Symptoms include:

Slight nutcase	*Avoidance of school, tendency to hide in wardrobes (curable)*
Moderate nutcase	*Tendency to throw chairs when given large amounts additive-filled orange juice (controllable)*
Severe nutcase	*Claims to have forgotten the prime minister (debatable)*

But Domino was more intelligent than the nurses and the teacher, and more intelligent than her join-the-dot-spots and pouty liver lips would have us all imagine. It was she who eventually worked it out about the reading.

Matchstick had attempted to escape from his taxi that morning and so was whisked away to be interrogated by Dr Doom; Domino and I had been told to do revision while Prune-face hovered over the hyper kids. Domino watched me flick through the pages of an anonymous pictureless textbook. She sat tapping her pencil for a few minutes before saying, 'You don't know what you're doing, do you?'
'This book's just boring that's all.'

'Have you read any of it?'

If I say 'yes' she'll say 'what's it about?', if I say 'no' she'll say 'how do you know it's boring?'

'I'm just skim-reading', I say, opting for the non-committal answer. I'd heard the mother say she'd skim-read a magazine and I thought it sounded quite intelligent.

'That's funny,' she said, snatching up my book, 'you're holding it upside down!'

Between them, Ruth and Domino showed me the basics of the alphabet.

a b c d e f g h i j k l m n o p q r s t u v w x y z

a the in on if of off out cat mat pat sat hat fat flat rat dog log bog hog shop stop pop cop mop drop ship sheep fish wish wash dish

The cat sat on the mat
The fat cat sat on the mat
The fat cat sat on the flat mat

I swallowed words with my eyes and within a month, I could read every word from the books that were prescribed for the hyper kids – even if what I was reading didn't really make any sense to me.

Flat Stanley is a boy who gets put inside envelopes
Flat Stanley is a book I have read
Flat Stanley is my favourite book
Flat Stanley is a boy who gets flattened

(*Flat Stanley* is a hilarious children's book about Stanley Lambchop, a normal healthy boy who is reduced to half an inch thick when a noticeboard falls on his head, squashing him. This is life-changing for Stanley and he finds he can go places and do all kinds of things, including being folded up and posted in an envelope.)

The writing was still a problem. I couldn't grasp how to hold a pencil and I could barely copy from a book, never mind compose words in my head. I could recognize words on a page but when it came to remembering what each letter looked like in my head, I'd often end up with an interesting zig-zaggy design or a new style of hieroglyphic.

The cat sat on the mat

The tt stt ff tthe tt

❧

An Ode to a Friend's Helping Hands

You drew with articulate talent, and
You held my hand when I couldn't even
Hold a pencil. I was secretly proud
That I, so ignorant and obscure had
Found a friend whose words were so beautiful
And, I felt incredibly vain that my

Awkwardness could ever be overlooked
By someone as graceful as you, Ruth. Then,
Your sweet sixteenth birthday came along and,
Among all the other cards, there was one
Written in a small childish hand which was
Mine. So, we wrote till we'd nothing left to

Write about – Then, somehow, we were lost for
Words. Three years passed and I often wished we'd
Shared more words. To hide my disappointment,
I wrote furiously and my writing
Improved, sloping backwards and forwards and
Then, that night, when you waved to me in the

Bar, you were still shining like the sunshine
In June. It was a colourful evening
And everyone looked so bright. You handed
Me a drink and told me you were proud of
Me for coming, and I promised you, I'd
Write – If you could still read my handwriting.

∂

On Wednesdays the centre is shut, so a home-help person comes to look after me. She's nice, I like her and she has a son who is the same age as me and a daughter who is in something called a *primarytu* (later, I learn that this child is in her second year of primary school). The mother knows her. She stays near us and her house is on my paper round.

I wish every day was Wednesday.

No one at the day unit talked about my disability and I wasn't supposed to ask questions. I didn't even know how to broach the subject and it was my imperfection. It happened to me. On the outside I still looked like an average child, but I thought people would magically see inside where I couldn't hide who I really was.

I don't know why but the home-help doesn't come any more on a Wednesday. Did I do something wrong? Nobody tells me anything.

I've been allocated another home-help. I like her, she is quirky and funny and talks about her grown up family. She is around fifty with dyed auburn hair and she wears Calvin Klein jeans. I still liked the other home-help better, though. Maybe they thought I wouldn't notice if they swapped my home-help for that other woman but I did.

I am not stupid. Them at the hospital place, I hate them.

⁓

criticize me They for my organization. lack my lack of memory and of I am having trouble memorizing objects the names of and I can't more remember than three new things at a Yesterday. , time I remembered what cutlery was but I can't tell the today difference and between fork knife. Sometimes when people speak to me, I recognize the clue, but words I don't have a what they mean.

I get lost get lost in conversation easily really easily. I get lost in especially if the person uses more than ten words in a row ten words in row I get lost if people keep saying lots of conversations or there's more more than more than one person talking. I forget what they told me two minutes ago. I am getting quite good at remembering people though. I am learning lots of people what they are called. And I know lots of people.

Chapter 3

Diagnosis

'Are you sure there was never any substance abuse?'

'NO! I told you this all happened overnight. She went out with her friends...'

'If you can't look after her then we can always send her to a home in Dumfries,' said Dr Doom. 'It's only sixty-six miles away.'

'Sixty-six miles,' gasped my mum, incredulously. 'How will I get to visit her?'

'There's good public transport!'

'She isn't the same Lynsey,' the mother trembled.

Bravo! Round of applause!

'I mean, I don't know what to do with her,' replied Dr Doom. 'It's all very bizarre.'

I was labelled a 'hypochondriac', a 'liar', a 'junkie' etc. The doctors kept telling me they could find 'nothing wrong with me', because I was unable to communicate to them about the collision. I could not remember any details. The staff at the behavioural unit decided they could do no more for me.

BECAUSE I WAS UNCOOPERATIVE:

But I didn't go to the home. Nine months post-injury, Doom decides to send me to a colleague who deals with 'severely disturbed adolescents'. Ironically, her colleague was also the chairperson of a support group for brain injury survivors and their carers. Within twenty minutes at the first session, he noticed that I got very agitated and distressed when asked to remember anything and I didn't seem to keep track of the conversation for longer than five minutes.

Finally someone believed that my problems were really caused by a medical condition and that I was NOT crazy. I was sent for a head injury evaluation and BINGO! There it was, the answer my family had been seeking for nearly a year. No parent wants to hear that their child has a head injury but, all the same, it was a huge relief. I was diagnosed with

MODERATE
　　　TO
　　　　SEVERE
　　　　　　DEFICITS
　　　　　　　　IN
　　　　　　　　　SEVERAL
　　　　　　　　　　　AREAS
　　　　　　　　　　　　OF
　　　　　　　　　　　　　COGNITIVE
　　　　　　　　　　　　　　　FUNCTIONING

Retrograde...anterior grade...post traumatic amnesia... That's what he says I've got...RAPT... That's how I'll remember it... I've got RAPT amnesia... Three amnesias all wrapped into one... Dr Marvel says it's 'very rare' to have all three... Sometimes, my mum says 'it's a rare night'... I think that means it's good... No one else has three amnesias... I wonder what an amnesia is?

Then came the CAT scan and the EEG and later the MRI:

I feel fun-ny. Funny money. Runny honey. The doctors had to give me dopey tablet-pill-things to swallow for me to go in the head-machine-thing 'cause I didn't like it the last time. It felt like they were putting me inside a washing machine and my head would get all sucked off.

Draining

A noose of emotions, tightens
Choking me.
My mind is awash with fears,
Provoking tears
To blind me.
Insanity is running amok
Through me.
Perplexed, like tangled socks
Imbedded in a mangled wash,
My feelings, spinning faster
Than a bastard typhoon
In a washing machine.

I'm like a stick of chalk
Trying to work, on a wet black board:
I'm whiter than white
And no one can see
Me.

I hang myself
Out to dry
After my good rinse.
My heart feels like a sponge
Inside a vice.
I want to cry,
Again

But, I am drained.
The dregs of my mind
Float like little spittals
Then self-dissolve,
Into my sorrow.

The tests were clear. 'No physical signs of brain abnormality.' They said that the circumstances surrounding my injury were too subtle and the tests would have to have been done straight after my accident to pick anything up. They said I could get another kind of test done but it would cost tens of thousands of pounds. I was supposed to get a portable thing like a personal stereo to take home but that never materialized either.

It all comes down to money. Why should I have to suffer? It was their mistake. Just because I have no scars or fractures doesn't mean my brain's not broken.

`'Brain damaged. Brain dead. Stupid. Vegetable.'`

Well, excuse me if I find that offensive.

`'People who have brain injuries slobber on them-`
`selves, wear giant nappies and cannot talk.'`

That's the general misconception of the public. Well, the doctors should have known better.

Anyway, I not only do NOT remember the accident but it also stole just over fourteen years worth of memory from me. So all I can go on is my friends', family's and doctors' renditions of what happened:

The theory was that

1. I was swinging on a chair.

2. I fell back and hit my head on a table behind me.

3. I fell to the floor and hit my head again.

4. Just for good measure I caught the table in front of me with my feet.

5. I pulled that down on my head as well!

❧

It was hard to carry on a conversation, especially in the first couple of years. I'd lose my train of thought

in the middle of a sentence and the slightest thing would distract me and I'd forget what I was

❧

Retrograde... Anterior grade... Post-traumatic amnesia... I'll remember that... Retrograde... Andorra what? ... Shit what was that second one again? ... Keep forgetting that word ... That's fucking stupid aphasia for you...

Aphasia = problems with word flooding... I mean...fighting...umm...finding

In cabbages...colleges...conversations I deviate often, going off on tangents rather than keeping to the topic at hand.

My alternating and divided attentions are very limiting.
There are so many times when I'm in a conversation and someone interrupts
and I

cannot think of where we were in conversation:

✈✓ ✗☞☞ ••◐✓♌⤳•• ☞✈☞✗ ✄<☮✈♌✗••✗ ✓◐ ⚇✗‼ ✈✓
✗☞☞ ••◐✓♌⤳•• ☞✈☞✗ ✄<☮✈♌✗••✗ ✓◐ ⚇✗‼‼‼ ✈✓
✗☞☞ ••◐✓♌⤳•• ☞✈☞✗ ✄<☮✈♌✗••✗ ✓◐ ⚇✗‼‼

Sometimes, it all just sounds like Chinese.

❧

'Difficulty processing and receiving information,' – how many times have I heard that line? The experts say that's where a lot of my problems stem from and that my attention and concentration deficits are merely symptoms of 'compromised mental efficiency'.

'A bit like a computer?' I think I'm beginning to catch onto some of the jargon.

'Yes, if you like. Have you heard of multitasking?'

'Is that when you can work on more than one document at a time?'

'Yes, that's right.'

I beamed, pleased that I had extracted something from my memory that I'd recently learned.

'Well, the brain's a bit like a computer,' continued the doctor, 'and sometimes when it's overloaded with information, it closes down.'

I was starting to get a headache. IS MY BRAIN CLOSING DOWN?

'For instance, if you are watching TV and someone starts a conversation –'

'I can't listen and watch at the same time.'

'Exactly, it's difficult for your brain to juggle more than one activity at a time.'

There's a phone ringing. I can't hear what he's saying. – Brr '– what' – Brrr '– do you think about' – Brrr brrr brrrring '?'

Noises annoy me.

Background noise annoys me when I'm watching the TV or studying. I can't read and listen. I can't sort out my CD collection and listen to music. I can't make toast and tea at the same time. I can't even organize my sock drawer and have a conversation.

'Do you want jam or butter on your toast?'

'Sssh,' I glare.

'Margaret,' the father persists, talking even louder, 'jam or butter.'

'Oh, I'll just have crackers and butter,' replies the mother.

'I've made toast now.'

'Can you shut it!'

'People have got to speak.'

'You're ruining it. You're making me miss it.'

'You've missed nothing.'

And I kept asking the parents the same question over, and over, and over again, since I could not remember asking it, nor the answer given. For a long time it was not possible for me to watch a thirty-minute television programme because I could not remember what was happening from one minute to the next or who any of the characters were. One good thing about having memory problems is, almost every film I've watched – no matter how many times I've seen it – it's like watching it for the first time.

Receiving, processing, storing, retrieving and expressing information:

_____involves the process of drawing on knowledge that has previously been stored. It forms the_____for all new_____. Retrieval of prior knowledge during_____, directly affects the amount of new_____that can be_____. Following a brain injury, survivors often have reduced levels of previous knowledge, hampering retrieval and, therefore, their_____to process new information.

[Knowledge, retrieval, processed, information, foundation, ability, learning]

❧

'How do you feel about staying in the adolescent unit for a few weeks? I'd like to monitor you as an inpatient,' said the nice doctor.

I don't like you anymore.

The parents and the not-nice doctor take me on a visit to the hospital-type-adolescent-unit-place.

I don't like it here.

It's raining; as we drive up, there's a woman laughing and rolling around on the grass.

What a stupid woman, she's not even wearing a hood.

Inside the dour-faced grey-brick building there is a long narrow corridor with bright pastel-crayoned pictures stickied all the way along the walls. A tea-trolley woman shuttles by with a big silver hot plate.
'This is the kitchen,' says the doctor.

Duh. I know what a kitchen is.

Down and along another skinny anaemic corridor, he points out the nurse's station. A troll-like-goatee-bearded-man pops his head out from round the door. I am told that he is to be my key worker.

Hmmph. I can see it all now: he's just going to be a hairier version of the Specimen.

Further down, there is a pay phone loosely attached to a wall and the bubble of soundproof glass surrounding it is cracked and graffitied.
'Patients are allowed to use the phone...'
Blah-blah blah-blah-blah... I wasn't listening anymore. I was watching the pretty blonde girl using the phone. Her hand trembled and shook and her eyes were red ringed with tears.

I wonder why she's here. She doesn't look mad.

'Yes, but...yes...no...I...' I could hear her gulping back the tears between words.

And she sounds quite posh.

'Lynsey, this will be your room over here...'

The parents and the doctor trolleyed me along to the end of the corridor. I was going to be living in a walk-in cupboard from now on and I had the joy of a bed, a wardrobe and a bare wooden desk. Oh, and I mustn't forget the handsome table lamp that looked as though it had been around since the eighteenth century.

My face feels hot and swollen as tears trickle down my cheeks. I watch the parents exchange furtive glances. I can't breathe, I can't think of anything to say.

Nobody wants me. I am a burden. I am an embarrassment. They are sending me away.

The skinny greasy-hair nurse with the bad breath asks me what I'd like to eat. I don't know.

Do I deserve lunch? Will they think I am greedy? Should I wait and see how long I can go without eating? Why am I even here?

Another nurse brings the meals on wheels. Other patients call it 'the shit truck'.

No prizes for guessing why. Everything is either yellow, brown or orange. Except the vegetarian meals which are green, grey and red, and border on gourmet by comparison.

I choose the vegetarian cannelloni, I've never tasted it before. At least, I don't think I have. The over-stuffed staff nurse with the cheeks like a gerbil and electric shock curls is a vegetarian. She takes a double-whammy portion. They give me chips, too.

Don't even want chips. Taste like cardboard. Hate the food. Hate the fat, hairy staff nurse. Hate this place. Maybe if I don't eat they

will take me home. Why am I here? What are they going to do to me? I feel like a lab rat. They are making me do things I don't want to do. If I could finally disappear for good then no one would have to look after me. No one would have to worry anymore. Everyone could move on, they'd be much happier.

æ

... There were doors all around the halls, but they were all locked; And Alice had been all the way down one side and up the other, trying every door, she walked sadly down the middle, wondering how she would ever get out again.

Alice's Adventures in Wonderland, Chapter 1

On my first day as an inpatient, I could not find my way back to my room. Too embarrassed to ask, I sat for about two hours in the TV and recreation room, flicking through magazines.

It's so *frustrating* when:

> you get lost even in the most familiar surroundings
> (e.g. can't find the toilet in your own house);
> when you go to the shops to buy one thing
> and end up coming home with something completely bizarre;
> or your memory is always
> crashing like a dodgy computer,
> so you're always forgetting people's...eyes...no...names, and...you...struggle
> to remember the phone numbers you dial on a regular basis.

It's *exhausting* when:

> you're always getting lost,
> or bumping into things,

walking into walls,
you would really like to do something…
but you get so fatigued by your head injury,
you have to give up almost as soon as you've begun;
or when you are searching for a…thing…a…brain…
a word
in your brain,
and the word that comes out is…
notice…nowhere…
nothing like the one you went…meant.

How did I get into the middle of the street?

Going outdoors can be stressful: supermarkets, busy shops, crowded restaurants, public transport, background noise, revolving doors, elevators and…fucking pigeons!

> Rats with wings attack
> Like mini pterodactyls
> Hunting a stale crust.

All pigeons are complete sociopaths. I hate the way they creep up on you and flap their ragamuffin wings two inches above your head, and the way they stare at you with their mean little curranty eyes.

Panic rushed through my mind. I wanted to scream but my throat was so dry, I felt like I'd just eaten an entire packet of Jacob's Cream Crackers. The mother stood at the checkout while she sent me back to get a loaf of bread she'd forgotten, on an aisle a few feet away. Then I'd wandered across to the next aisle
to look at something else.
Now I was lost.

I hurried from bakery to cold meat.

'Mum, where are you?' I panicked. 'How am I going to get home?'

I   felt isolated in a busy shop full of strangers.

I'd felt that way so much in the nine months since November 1992 (I can never remember the exact date). I was an outsider in my own life.

I couldn't remember myself.

After what seemed like hours, I found the mother at the checkout, exactly where I'd left her a few minutes earlier.

'Where's my loaf, Lynsey?'

I'd forgotten the bread.

Occasionally, I still have nightmares about getting lost in the supermarket, or getting locked in after closing time.

Chapter 4

The Mental Hospital, Rebellion + Bullying

'It was much pleasanter at home,' thought poor Alice, 'when one wasn't always growing larger and smaller, and being ordered about by mice and rabbits. I almost wish I hadn't gone down that rabbit-hole – and yet – and yet – it's rather curious, you know, this sort of life! I do wonder what can have happened to me!'

Alice's Adventures in Wonderland, Chapter 4

I had resigned myself to thinking that I would be stuck in a cupboard at the adolescent unit forever. I started making over 'my room' before the end of my second day. Not content with decorating the walls with movie and pop posters, I insisted that the parents bring over my hi-fi and my own duvet.

'The girl next door has got a 'Snatch the dog' bed cover.'

'Ok, but I don't think you need your hi-fi.'

'I do so, the girl next door has a hi-fi.'

'You're not going to be here for very long.'

'Well, I want it and I want it now,' I said, 'don't come back to visit me without it.'

There were eight inpatients in total: the Princess, the Vampire, the Anorexic girl, the Posh girl, the Hypochondriac, Hamster-boy, the Giggler and me. Then there were the day patients: the Vegetarian girl (she was the main reason for the gourmet meals), the Computer-geek (who didn't speak apart from shouting obscenities every time he lost his Super Mario powers) and the Wolf-boy who was growing a beard and used to be an inpatient before I came to stay at the unit and got his old room.

Occasionally, we had 'floaters' who only came in for an out-patient appointment once a month or came in on emergency overnight stay: like the Junkie-girl who was 'jellied' – who everyone else (especially the vampire and the princess) was scared of.

> I thought she was really nice. She seemed really happy and cheery compared to this lot, in here.

The Princess lived next door to me.

> She's got everything: her own bedcover, a hi-fi and thirty-seven CDs, TV, video, fourteen sweater shop jumpers and twelve pairs of dressy shoes and a pair of caterpillar boots.

'I want caterpillar boots.'

> She's got teddies and ornaments and a beanbag and her own lamp to match her bedcovers...

At home, I had to share a room with the sister. I felt that she was always looking at me, watching me and telling me not to touch her stuff or telling me to tidy up and put my things away.

> MY THINGS? What things do I own? This is the other Lynsey's room. EVERYTHING belongs to her: HER bed, HER furniture, HER games and HER books.

I liked some of her books – I had to admit, she had good taste.

'Mum, are those my books?' I asked when I noticed the bedroom bookshelf was choked from top to bottom with stories such as *Alice in Wonderland* and *The Chronicles of Narnia*. It was so embarrassing to be so old and yet feel so young. I was fifteen years old and I couldn't write simple sentences. I was so happy I could now read, but I couldn't remember *what* I'd read.

I since and sense make didn't things ,naturally so left to right from reading was I .anyway matter didn't it ,sentence the of end the to got I before forget would

In fact, I taught my sister how to say her name and address backwards.

We had a computer. A computer that talked when you typed in words. A computer that once upon a time the other Lynsey taught her little sister how to play. Now, the little sister had taken over the role as the big sister:

'What are you doing, stupid?'

'What?'

'You're putting the disk in backwards,' she scolded, 'Mum, tell her – she's going to end up breaking this.'

I am going to read EVERY book in this cupboard. I am going to be a better reader than HER. One day, I'll become a writer – I WILL – and I'll write my own book and I'll be much smarter and better-er than SHE ever was.

UTOPIA

The library is my sanctuary:
I rather prefer books to people.
I secrete myself mid their concrete
Pages like a neat leather marker.

I seek refuge from this wordless life,
From characters so bland and austere.
I slip quietly beneath the sheet
Of another world, covering my

Burning ears. With pleasure, my hollow
Eyes devour whole sentences like fare
But my parchment thin ideals share the
Thin air that only heroines breathe.

*'There ought to be a book written about me, that there ought! And
when I grow up, I'll write one – but I'm grown up now,' she added in
a sorrowful tone; 'at least there's no room to grow up any more here.'*

Alice's Adventures in Wonderland, Chapter 4

'Don't be ridiculous,' said the gerbil-faced staff nurse, 'What do you
want to write an autobiography at your age for.'

'That's nice,' said the mother, 'I'll buy you a diary for Christmas.
You can put your poems in it.'

'Very good,' says the father.

Somehow, I don't think they know what I'm talking about.

In sixth year, in high school, I toyed with the idea once again.

'Calderwood,' snarled the freckled-face Ferret-boy in my class,
'Who'd want to read a book about you?'

'Lynsey,' chastised the teacher, 'I think you should get your head
out of the clouds and concentrate on your studies.'

Why can't I write a book? I've got lots of things to write about.

Alone. So alone. We are all here together in the family therapy
session but I feel so isolated from everyone. I am sitting as far apart as
possible in one corner of the box room. The sister is boohooing in
the opposite corner. The psychologist-nurse-thingummy-woman
with the big mad hair has given her coloured pens and a big white
sheet of paper to draw on.

The first time I met the mad-hair-thingummy-woman she had
shiny silver blonde hair slicked back into a ponytail and was wearing
black jodhpurs and a white starched shirt with a slim tie. A few days

later, I was summoned to her room only to find a stranger who was wearing a long cream skirt and a vest top and had cotton candy pink hair in loose light waves.

Pink hair! She's got pink hair like candyfloss. This is the person who's supposed to take our family meetings?

Family meeting:

Once a week or once a whatever, depending on the individual family, the parents and the children get together with a psychiatrist or psychologist to rant and shout at each other. Most of the time I can't concentrate, so I just go to sleep.

Just before I met with the parents and the sister for the next family meeting, I tried to tell the mother. 'See that woman,' I said.
 'What woman?'
 'That woman that takes us for the family meeting thing.'
 'What about her?'
 'She's got pink hair.'
 'Don't be ridiculous.'
 As soon as we walked into her little comfy-seat room with the round table, the mother and father exchanged glances.
 'That's a different woman!'
 The mad-hair-thingummy-woman's hair was now straight, short and plum-coloured.
 Later, she says, 'Don't you ever just give Lynsey a huge hug?'
 'She doesn't like that,' answers the mother (too quickly).

How do you know? Have you ever tried? Horrible, you think I'm horrible. I am horrible. Horrible and greedy and I can't do anything right.

I sit growling and pouting in the corner.

'Can you tell us what is bothering you, Lynsey?'

I want to announce that I do like hugs but instead I shriek, 'You don't love me!'

'If we didn't love you then we wouldn't be here,' protests the mother.

'No, you don't love me. You love HER.'

Everyone assumed I was talking about Nikki. They thought I was jealous of her – well, I was to a certain extent. She had taken on the role of the big sister, she was trying to teach me all the things that I had taught her in the past. But I was confused and angry and I didn't possess the communication skills to explain that I WASN'T talking about her.

'We don't love you any less,' the parents protested.

'Huh, you don't love me. You just love your darling daughter,' I ranted.

'Yes, Nicola is our darling daughter. You both are.'

'Well, I'm sick of hearing about your darling daughter and how perfect she was.'

How perfect she was. How perfect I had been. I was sick of hearing about what I used to be like. How much I'd changed. How could I compete? So I walked out following that tirade of abuse. I don't know what else was said but I know that it was enough to make the sister refuse to ever come to another family therapy session.

I never dreamed of HER. I simply couldn't remember anything about the person I used to be. But the disappointment is always there just under the surface, of what I could have been. I had no idea what was going on. I had trouble dealing with everything. No one could understand. Not even myself.

Troll-thing, the psychiatric nurse who was my key worker, he said I was depressed.

What does he know? He's just a fat hairy freak anyway. He thinks he looks like Jason Orange but he's ten times uglier. I hate Jason Orange. He's the ugliest one out of *Take That*.

'I'm recommending that you stay here with us for another month.'

I didn't care. Didn't care anymore. I couldn't cope at home. I couldn't cope going back at the weekends, when I'd argue with the family. Then they'd send me back and nothing would be resolved.

I want to stay. Stay here, where it's safe. The same routine.

Brain injuries rob you of the most basic skills that most people take for granted. They can alter personalities. They can erase memories.

'What if she never remembers any of us?'

They talk about me as if I'm not here half the time. I'm here. I can hear you. But I'm telling you nothing. Nothing from now on. NOTHING.

My parents have told me that dealing with the 'loss' of my memory felt 'worse than a bereavement'.

I often felt in the early days that it would've been easier if I'd just died. 'Some days,' the mother told the psychologist, 'I wish a bomb would land on our house and blow us all up.' There were old photographs of the other Lynsey and the sister all round the house but I made them take them all down. 'She doesn't like to look at herself,' said the mother. 'We try to show her pictures but she just throws them back in our face.'

That's because it's not me.

'She used to be her daddy's girl but now she won't even talk to him.' The father sits, hunched over, hanging on the mother's every word. 'Is that right, Mr Calderwood?' The psychologist woman had been trying to bring him into the conversation but his input only ever stretched as far a 'yes,' 'no' and random jerks with his head and shoulders. I was cold, clinical. I detached myself emotionally. I made no attempt to bond with this new instant family. 'What if she never remembers herself?'

I AM MYSELF.

YOU DON'T EVEN KNOW ME.

&

7:00 a.m.   The day staff arrive. Twenty-storey-high plates of freshly made toast float past my room and all the way down the corridor to the nurse's station.

8:00 a.m.   The Vampire's med time. She gets a cocktail of tablets every six hours. They have to watch her like a hawk to make sure that she is swallowing them. She told me she used to hide them under her tongue and store them in the back of her wardrobe till the end of the week, then she'd swallow the lot and get a high.

The Vampire was the first inmate I met. Our first encounter was when a young student nurse partially introduced us, on my first day.

'And this is –'

'I want a word with you,' seethed the Vampire, baring her revolting yellow teeth. I couldn't help but notice, they were long and pointed like Count Dracula's. Her ice blue eyes were watery and her tiny pin dot pupils were floating like little minuscule lily pads.

Is she talking to me?

Her fist shot out like a hammer on a spring.

Oh, don't hit me.

The student managed to catch her hand.

'Fucking cow,' she raved, 'fucking smelly cow.'

She hadn't been aiming at me, after all. Apparently, the student had suggested to her earlier that she should take a shower and this was some kind of delayed reaction. 'Fucking skinny, smelly cow. Take a fucking shower yourself,' she screamed, as they trolleyed her away. Later, when the staff asked me how I was settling in, I said, 'Fine.'

Fucking fine.

The Vampire was the same age as me but with her height and incredible girth, she towered above me like an ogre. She had been at the adolescent unit for three years, aside from the occasional holiday in the IPCU (intensive psychiatric care unit). Apparently, she couldn't cope there as she was the youngest and she found the other patients 'too intimidating'.

9:30 a.m.   School. I didn't mind going to lessons. In fact, I couldn't wait to get to real school.

The Vampire never came to class. She slept most of the day and prowled through the night. I used to watch her through the eye of my room, wandering round like a sleepwalker, eyes all puffed up and red.

I am alone. Hopelessly alone in this cold, miserable shoebox of a room. I'm frightened and I can't sleep. I can hear the Vampire shambling up and down the corridor like a zombie.

Shuffle, shuffle, scuffle, muffle

She's stopped. I can hear her ghoulish voice reverberating round my skull like a boomerang. Shivering, I slip out of bed and press my nose hard against the glass (they like to keep to the curtain open so they can watch you).

She's talking to HER on the night staff. I bet she's allowed to stay up and watch *Prisoner: Cell Block H*. She always gets special treatment just because they can't control her. She shouldn't even be here. She ought to be in IPCU. How do they expect me to sleep when that psychopath is running around loose? She's already attacked the Hypochondriac girl.

I hated the way she crept around like the walking dead, in the early hours of the morning. I was too scared to even go to the toilet in case I met her.

I wish they would lock my door so she can't get in.

The Princess told me that one time she cut someone's throat when they were sleeping. She says I should watch out in case she comes in and murders me in my bed.

❧

'Your mother is a fucking moany old bag,' said the Princess.

'I know. She doesn't let me do anything.'

'That's a shame,' the Anorexic girl piped up, all angelic. 'I think your mum's really nice.'

Hmmmph.

'You're lucky she comes to visit you at all. My mum can only manage…'

Hmmmph.

'I'm not sitting listening to this pish,' sulked the Princess, 'I'm going for a fag.'

I shrugged and followed the Princess into the smoking room. Inpatients were allowed to smoke as long as they had parental permission. The Princess and the Vampire smoked like chimneys. There were four burnt orange leather chairs, decorated with cigarette burns. Some of the yellow stuffing was spewing out of the chairs and I liked to pick it and roll the spongy stuff between my fingers.

'I thought you were banned from smoking?'

'So fuck. What are they going to do, lock me up?'

'My mum lets me smoke. It's my dad that's the fucking boring bastard.'

'My mum would kill me.'

'Probably. You're just like little Miss Perfect out there, too shit scared to try anything that would upset the parents.'

'What does it taste like?'

'What?'

'Cigarettes.'

'Try it for yourself.'

She stretched out her arm, teasing me with the smouldering white stick.

'Oh, I don't know.'

'Why don't you go and ask skeleton-features, out there, if she thinks you should try it?'

'Do you think so?'

I started, enthusiastically, towards the door.

'Oh, you are such a dick.'

I sucked, gently; the curls of grey smoke tickled my tongue. The Princess had already 'sparked up' another and was artistically blowing rings of smoke in the air. I noticed that she always cocked her head to the side before she did this, closed one eye. I tried to copy her but the smoke came out in balls and lumps instead of pretty little rings.

'What the fuck you doing?'

'Trying to make bubbles.'

'Bubbles?'

'What you're doing.'

'You're not even fucking inhaling it to start with.'

'Oh.'

I sucked harder. Dragging the warm, thick fumes into the back of my throat:

COUGH

COUGH

COUGH COUGH COUGH COUGH

The Princess was laughing so much she didn't even see the Anorexic-girl's red head bobbing up and down at the glass partition.

CRE-EAK

'You two girls should not be in here.'

It was Gerbil-features, who had come to see what all the noise was.

'This will be reported to your key workers.'

'Big fucking whoopee do,' muttered the Princess.

'Your parents have already raised the issue that they do not want you smoking.'

The Anorexic-girl shrugged in a 'what could I do' type of fashion as we were hustled back to our rooms. We all knew that this would be the exciting topic of conversation at tomorrow's lunchtime community meeting.

12:00 a.m.	Community meeting. A run-down of what happened yesterday. A good time to run the place down. One person reads the 'minutes' from the previous day and someone else takes notes for the present day. Depending who was writing the minutes, it could be really mundane or really obscure.

14 September

A new girl arrived. Posh girl is on pass. Wolf-boy is going back to school. Tomorrow night is supper group and it's the Vampire's turn to go supper group shopping.

15 September

The food in here is crap. The Vampire thinks we should get a Chinese takeaway for supper group. Evening community meeting should be scrapped so that we can watch Neighbours on the telly. The girls want to swap toilets with the boys because they have got marble sinks and bigger mirrors.

Hamster-boy was the only boy inpatient. He lived in the room diagonally opposite me. When he first moved in, he was as timid as a mouse. He didn't even go to the community meeting. He went straight to his room and no one saw him for days. His lamp would be burning away at night and I could hear scratching noises coming from behind his door.

He looks too innocent to be another vampire

His door was lying ajar and there was a yellow light spewing into the corridor. All I could hear was

Scritch – scratch – rittle-rattle

I'd never heard anything like it. I'd never seen anything like it. It was huge. Reddish brown with a creamy white stripe on its back. A ginormous hamster that was bigger than my hand and could leap off the side of hamster-boy's bed. Her name was Blanche. And she was pregnant.

Blanche had five babies but she ate three of them. I didn't like Blanche after that. Hamster-boy gave me one of the other babies. She was a tiny reddish bundle of fluff with the same creamy stripe as her mum. A mini Blanche. A little pipsqueak. I called her 'Pip'.

I liked to put Pip in my shirt pocket and carry her around, but not for too long in case she got bored and took it upon herself to go for a sky dive. The parents got me a metal cage with an exercise wheel and a salt wheel for her teeth, a ball to run around in outside and a cube shaped tunnel with lots of holes she could weave in and out of.

Animal hair irritated the mother's asthma but she liked Pip. She liked to watch Pip run along the corridor in her wheel and she brought her lots of hamster burgers and sunflower seeds and other treats.

When the Giggler came to the unit, she joined the hamster club as well. The Giggler used to put her hamster on the pool table and let him rendezvous with the balls. Spike was a grey, longhaired hamster with a long skinny body and fuzzy white whiskers. We had to be careful in case he disappeared down any of the pockets, thinking they were mouse holes.

It was around that time that the Vampire decided that she wanted a hamster. I didn't like her touching Pip, in case she strangled her. Anytime the Vampire saw me with Pip, I'd just say 'I'm just putting her back in her house because she needs the toilet.'

So Hamster-boy got his dad to bring 'Blinky' back to the unit. Blinky was the remaining baby hamster who had only one eye. He was a mousey brown colour but had that trademark white stripe down his back just like all the rest of Blanche's children.

I knew she couldn't look after a hamster. She can't look after herself.

She was always feeding Blinky stupid unhamsterish foods like cheese and crisps and cold pizza and, she was always leaving the cage door open. That's why I wasn't surprised when I heard Blinky had gone AWOL.

'He's out! He's escaped, I saw him!'

Who's escaped? Someone from the ICPU? Another of your hallucinations? Pity you don't try and escape, no such luck.

I was sitting playing *Super Mario Bros* on the computer in the day room and the vampire was staring at the floor in front of the TV. I'd learnt to ignore her tantrums and hallucinations. When she saw things there was nothing anyone else could do and I was scared she might lash out at me if I tried to calm her down.

'Aaaaaah a spider! A big giant hairy spider!'

'Where?'
'It's on the wall.'

'Kill-it, kill-it,' she screamed, 'kill-it-kill-it-kill-it.'

'I can't see it.'
Giggle-giggle.
The Princess was throwing back her head and blowing minty smoke halos with menthol cigarettes, up at the ceiling.
'I can't see a spider.'

'AAAAAAAAAAARRRRRRGGGGGGHHHH'

The Vampire flew out of the smoking room, flapping her arms like bat wings.
'Daft bitch,' laughed the Princess, 'she's fucking seeing things.'
Later, the Vampire came to visit me in my room.
'Hi, are you feeling better?'
'What do you mean?'

Gerbil-features had said she wasn't feeling well.

'Fucking talking about me? Fucking laughing at me?'

'No, I was just –'

'You fucking seen what she got for laughing at me.'

She pointed through the gap in the half-closed door at the Hypo-chondriac girl who'd just disappeared into her room with the Giggler and a plate of toast. The bruise on her cheek was beginning to turn yellow, yet she still walked with a limp (however, whether it was a real limp was debatable as the Princess said she'd seen her changing legs from time to time).

THWACK

She smacked the left side of my cheek with the back of her hand.

'Fucking don't start with me,' she snarled, as she turned and stalked out into the corridor.

Scritch-scratch. Rittle-rattle

'In there, in there, I heard it!'

It was about 2 a.m. that morning and there was a commotion in the kitchen. I woke to witness the nursing staff with plastic gloves and aprons, raking through the bins under the instruction of the Vampire.

She's probably hearing things. How could Blinky get in the bin?

It turned out that someone had left a cupboard door open directly behind the bin and he'd crept inside. From that moment on, hamsters were kept in the day room.

❧

'Your hair wants cutting,' said the Hatter.

Alice's Adventures in Wonderland, Chapter 7

The nurses were releasing me overnight because it was the night of my school dance and the mother had to take me for an emergency hair saving operation.

'Remember,' teased the hairdresser, 'Hairdressers cut hair.'

It was all the Princess' fault. She was the one. The one that cut my hair.

I had been trying to grow my hair. It was short, thick and shrub-like and my fringe had grown right down to my nose. The Vampire called me 'Hedge Hopper'. It was really the Princess who thought the name up. She said it as a joke and then the Vampire latched onto it and used it at every available opportunity.

'Hey, Hedge Hopper! Have you seen the film Edward Scissorhands?'

GIGGLE

And the Princess, she made scissor gestures with her fingers every time she saw me.

'Why don't you just let her cut it?' said the Anorexic girl.

I shook my head.

'Fucking scaredy cunt,' snarled the Vampire.

'She cut our hair,' reasoned the Anorexic girl, 'and it's ok.'

And so she had. The Princess had trimmed both the anorexic-girl and the Vampire's fringe. It was only when she sprayed water on her own fringe that it jumped up, leaving her with an extra inch of forehead.

Finally, I gave in. 'But just the fringe,' I said.

SNIP SNIP SNIPPETY-SNIP

GIGGLE

'What are you laughing at?'

SNIP SNIP SNIPPETY-SNIPPETY-SNIPPETY-SNIP

GIGGLE

'I SAID, WHAT ARE YOU LAUGHING AT?'

SNIP-SNIP SNIP-SNIP

'I said, just do the fringe.'

'I am,' reassured the Princess, 'I'm just evening it up for you at the back.'

GIGGLE

'What's so funny?'

'Finished.'

'How does it look?'

'Oh...lovely.'

'You look like...'

'A burst couch,' hooted the Vampire.

AHAHAHAAHAHAHAHAHAHAHAHAHAHAH

'Youse are totally bastards,' snapped the Anorexic girl.

'My hair!'

'It's not that bad,' soothed the Anorexic girl. 'It looks ok from the back.'

'Yeah, pity about the front,' said the Vampire, 'looks like you've been attacked by a hedge cutter.'

'Now,' interjected the Princess, 'we can call you 'Hedge Clipper'!

AHAHAHAHAHAHAHAHAHAHAHAHAHAHA

SNIP

SNIP-SNIP

'I'm afraid that's the best I can do,' said the hairdresser. 'You'll just have to wait till it grows back.'

I'm never talking to them again.

I stared at my bald forehead in the mirror.

What I need is some kind of fringe wig.

Princess...fucking high and mighty...whatshername? Whatever did I see in her? I thought she was 'so fucking wonderful' as my mother so politely put it. I did too. I thought she was the fucking bees knees.

I remember thinking she was pretty – and I wished I looked like her. But now I have no recollection of her face. I keep squinting inside my mind to see if I can get a picture of what she looked like. I remember she had long dark hair and I know she had a fringe because of that time when she cut it herself and it ended up too short. I keep scratching at the back of my brain for some scant details but there's nothing. At times like this I wish I'd never burnt the stupid letters that she sent me when we got out. Back home, I sat, gloating over the charred remains of the Princess' letters. I just wanted to forget all about the Princess and her tricks. I just wanted to forget all about the hospital.

I'm never going back there. Never.

Now I wish I'd held onto all my memories of the hospital. Even though few of them were pleasant.

I hate it here. The Princess is a liar and she's not my friend anymore; the Anorexic girl is getting worse, she's in her bed most of the time and I'm only allowed to see her for half an hour each day; the Posh girl is away home, Giggles and the Hypochondriac don't talk to anyone except each other; Hamsterboy doesn't talk to anyone and the Vampire – well, I'd rather talk to four walls.

Pip was all I had left.

'Pi-ip,' I called her as if she was a dog. 'Pip-py!'

I wanted to take her home with me at the weekend. The parents said, 'No.'

'Fine then, I'll just stay here with Pip.'

And the moany staff...and the Vampire...I don't want to stay here but I don't want to leave Pip with them.

I'd been getting on better with the parents since I stopped talking to the Princess.

'Come on, Lynsey,' said the father, 'don't spoil it.'

'I'll look after your hamster,' said Troll-thing.

'There you are,' smiled the father. 'Pip will be fine.'

Reluctantly, I'd gone home. In fact, I had a great weekend, saw my friends, and the parents took me to the cinema. Now, I was back, I was desperate to see if Pip had eaten the chocolate hamster drops and the radish that I had left. I peeked through the little arched hole of her mousey house. She wasn't there. 'Where are you hiding, silly hamster?'

I scanned the inside of the cage: her food dish had been left untouched; her water bottle was leaking but still three quarters full, and there was Pip, lying at the foot of the little metal hamster stairs, wrapped in a cottony wool ball of hamster bedding.

Like a little hamster-angel.

'Wake up, sleepy.' I rattled the bars of the cage.

'Wake up!' I was beginning to get annoyed.

I've waited all this time to see you and I've even been to the pet shop to look for a new house and you can't even be bothered getting out of your bed to say 'hello'.

On closer inspection, I noticed that her hair was damp and matted with sawdust, the water bottle had dribbled onto her head.

I knew Pip was dead. I knew before I even touched her cold rigid body; before I even opened the cage door. I prodded her. First with a lollipop stick that had been lying on my desk and then with my finger.

No. No no no no noooo.

I didn't want Pip to be dead. Pip wasn't allowed to be dead. I'd never known anyone who was dead before. Other people died.

Why did you have to go and do this to me, Pip? Why did you have to go and stupid old die? Who's going to be my friend now?

❧

The first time I ever induced vomiting was when I was an inpatient in the hospital. That horrible night, I ate more chocolate biscuits than I could ever remember. I ate them because I could, I ate them because they were there, I ate them because there was no one to stop me. Eating in secret made me feel clever.

I binged on Fruit Club biscuits, my favourite, everyone's favourite (later, when I counted the wrappers there were 18 of them). One of the day patients stole a box of them when she was an inpatient, and kept them in her wardrobe.

Hamster-like, I crammed every last crumb into my bulging, chocolatey cheeks and until my abdomen was bursting, but biscuits couldn't fill the emptiness that I felt. Disgusted, I glared at my reflection in the mirror, stripped down to my underwear (I had drawn the curtain so no one could see in).

Greedy pig. Fat greedy pig.

I made myself sick. For the remainder of my stay in the adolescent unit this became fairly ritualistic. I'd wake up early in the morning and creep down to the kitchen. Fruit Clubs. Fruit Clubs. It always had to be the Fruit Club biscuits with the purple wrappers. It was easy sneaking fruit clubs from the biscuit tin. I had pockets in my pyjamas and huge furry slippers that I stuffed with chocolate biscuits – I learnt to walk without crushing them.

I felt powerful, as if I was getting one over on the nurses, and when the challenge of Club biscuits proved too easy, I progressed to anything that had a wrapper. Soon, I was claiming any left-over food in the fridge as my midnight entrees. I collected sweet wrappers like trophies. I would iron them out with a ruler then secrete them inside a patent black folder. As the folder became fatter, I became more obsessed with food and I began cutting pictures of food, and people who were eating, out of magazines.

When I was discharged, I emptied the folder of its contents.

I have to be more careful.

The Princess caught me unaware one night and I slapped the folder shut. A small scrap of paper fluttered onto the floor and she snatched it up before I could stop her.

'What's this?'

'Nothing, can I have it back?'

She sneered in disgust, 'You're not a lesbo are you?'

She waved the picture of a model eating ice cream in front of me like a carrot.

'No,' I replied, defensively. I didn't know what a 'lesbo' was but I didn't want to be one.

'Why are you collecting pictures of women then?'

This was my secret and I wanted it all to myself. I didn't want anyone to interfere or take it away from me. I liked this game. It was all about disguises and keeping up appearances.

I could just pretend to be Lynsey; they would never know the difference.

Chapter 5

Back to School + More Bullying

No one knew the extent of my injuries, and I didn't realize the severity of my memory loss, until after I returned to school. People were in and out of the house, visiting and wanting to coax my memory into reviving the old times. They brought out one hilarious anecdote after the other but I realized I didn't have anything to say.

'Oh do you remember that time we were...'

'Or what about the time when...'

'Oh c'mon, you must remember Rainbow.'

'No.'

'George? Zippy? Bungle?'

'No, I said I didn't.'

'George was a pink hippo with big long eyelashes.'

In the hospital school, for arts and crafts class, I'd made a hippo model using a metal stencil filled with crystal-thingies that melted and smoothed over like a stained glass window when you baked them in the oven. There were lots of different colours of crystals and we were supposed to share them, but I was determined that my hippo was going to be colour co-ordinated.

Her hippo looks stupid. It's got a blue face, yellow eyes, red toes and a green bum.

'Oi, you're taking all the pink!'

'I'm making a pink hippo.'

'Why can't you use another colour?'

'I am, I'm making its eyelids purple.'

'It looks like that big gay George from Rainbow.'

'Who?'

'Oh, you must be a freak if you don't remember Rainbow.'

'I think she fucking lives somewhere over a rainbow.'

Ha ha, I've seen *The Wizard Of Oz*, actually.

'Oh you must remember Rainbow!'

Well, no, I don't actually. Can we talk about something else? Ho-hum, bor-ing.

I sat in stony silence as they reviewed: their childhood, my child-hood, people I'd never heard of, places I'd never been – *I* never did any of these things. At least, not in this lifetime. Maybe the other Lynsey had been part of this but I WASN'T EVEN BORN THEN!

When are people going to learn that I can't remember what happened before I was fourteen? That means: no history; no TV programmes; no nursery rhymes; no bible stories; *nothing* that happened before the year 1992. DUH!

I tried to appear interested at first but it's a bit like listening to your granny rattle on about the olden days and the great-grand-cousins who died before your parents were even conceived.

I'd nod my head, crack a smile.

'Mmm, yeah, great...whatever...'

I could never be part of the conversation. I could feel the frustra-tion twisting like a knife as they tried to hack into my brain. I wanted to run, hide under the table, morph into the floor and slide under someone's shoe where no one could see my clumsy existence.

❧

I nearly walked right past her. I didn't even notice her. Why would I?

I was tired.

I was with the father and he'd been helping me with my paper round, Lynsey's paper round. The paper round that I'd inherited. I'd get lost if I had to deliver them on my own. That was the last of them. Two hundred and seventy-three papers and for most of them, I had to go up three or four flights of stairs. I was carrying my big orange paper bag; it was nearly as big as me.

A strange girl grabbed me by the strap of my bag. 'Lynsey!' She shrieked in my earhole. Acting like she'd not seen me in two hundred million years. Stunned, I stared right in at her face. My eyes were flashing like zoom lens, trying to devour her every feature.

'Don't you recognize me?'

She told me her name and straggled into the house behind us. Next, she battered into an epic about school and third-year exams, hitting me with a barrage of names I didn't even know and how was I getting on?

'Me? Fine.'

I don't like her poking into my mind for information. But she says we are friends. She says she sits next to me in class. I know there is something...something not quite right. But I've not got any other friends. No one else comes to see me.

Her face was red and she looked like she was about to take an asthma attack and she didn't seem satisfied with any of my answers. I had wanted to please her, answer all her questions but I just didn't know what she wanted to hear.

'You're not going away already?'

'I need to get going,' she said, stiffly, standing up.

'Oh, when will I see you again?'

She smiled, weakly at me, 'We'll see.' That was all she said: 'We'll see.'

We'll see. We'll see. We'll see.

I knew. I knew. I just knew I wasn't going to see her again. She wouldn't even let me walk her to the bus stop with my dad.

'I don't like that girl,' the mother said, when she was gone. 'She seemed to be just looking for information.'

I was wrong.

I did see her again.

The next time I saw her, I was back at school; she was standing with a group of girls and they were whispering and laughing.

They are laughing at me.

WSSSA WSSSA WSSSA WSSSA WSSSA WSSA

'...Her over there...' Giggle-giggle, giggle giggle. '...says she's lost her memory...'

But how could I expect fourteen and fifteen year olds to understand when adults were just as immature?

Lynsey had a friend, once. A friend who came to the house. A friend she went to school with. A friend she ate lunch with. Lynsey's friend didn't like me. Her parents didn't like me. 'Get rid of that girl,' they said, 'she's weird.' They didn't understand. They didn't want to understand. They were embarrassed. Affronted. At least that's the way I see it.

I'd hear the mother mentioning her name in whispers. Praying that she'd call. That she'd be my friend again. When I went back to school, I sought out the friend.

'Hi, I – I feel a bit funny saying this but –'

SIGH

'I mean,' I stammered, 'umm...'

'A-hem.'

'You used to be my friend...'

SIGH.

Three years later, my mum was at a brain injury support group and a man nervously entered. It was his first time at the group. His wife had been in road traffic accident. She suffered swelling to the brain. She wasn't the same person anymore. When her injuries healed, she looked the same. When the scars healed, there were no bruises or fractures, no bandages around her head and no magic wand to reveal her imperfections. His seventeen-year-old daughter wasn't coping. He told the group that her friend had had a brain injury three years before.

'I always said that all the ones that made a fool of you would get their come-uppance.'

'Right mum,' I sighed. 'Can you not just forget about her?'

'Just goes to show, you never know what's round the corner.'

SIGH.

I've seen that girl on the street and she just walks past me. So many times I've thought about walking over to her, offering my support, even throwing my arms around her. I've no idea why. I don't even know her. She doesn't even know me.

✑

It still happens even now, though not as often. I'll meet someone and they'll start talking to me and I'll have no idea who they are.

Michael.

Michael K.

Now, that was a name I hadn't heard in a long time.

If it was him? Must've been.

I saw the way he looked at me when I got on that train, with those hopeful, enquiring eyes of his.

Then I blanked him.

Sat in the next carriage.

It was the longest fifteen-minute journey of my life. All the way along the track, I could feel those bright blue eyes of his, boring into the back of my skull like laser beams.

And I kept trying to place him.

Trying to remember who the…

MICHAEL. MICHAEL K.

That was his name. I'd ask my parents when I got home. About him. About the past. About him and the past. Then again, maybe not. It might get their hopes up. They might think I'd remembered something.

Had I remembered something?

Or was it a pretend memory?

WHO was Michael K, anyway?

And did I really want to know?

Did I really?

I jerked back to life as if someone had thrown a bucket of ice water down my top. The train had stopped.

I almost missed my stop. Tripping over my bag, I searched for his eyes as I was leaving but he'd vanished like a ghost and so had the half

'Hey, Calderwood!'

I snapped back into consciousness.

How long have I been sitting here and how much conversation have I missed?

'Hey, memory woman! Can you not remember your own name?'

I could feel my cheeks burning with anger and embarrassment but I knew if I retaliated then things would just be made worse and my *friends* would turn the other cheek, scared in case they were ridiculed for associating with the school freak.

'MO-RON,' he said, wearily. 'You – need – to – move – your – fuck-ing – bag – so – I – can – get – past.'

I just stared.

'Are you brain dead or something?'

A red-headed girl walking past said, 'You're sad.'

I raked my thoughts to remember her name.

'Sad bastard. Fuck off.'

I felt a huge sigh of relief as the freckle-faced bully-boy swaggered off in the opposite direction.

'Thanks,' I smiled, weakly.

She swivelled round, grinning, 'Do you remember me?'

SIGH.

I was 'the new Lynsey'. I was childish, inadequate, incapable of filling my predecessor's shoes. Well, I was going to shock everyone. I was going to be different. I was going to establish an identity separate from the other Lynsey.

School just wasn't what I'd imagined it to be like: like in Maths, I just could not see the point in discussing the finer points of an isosceles triangle; I couldn't understand what they were angling at with all that acute and obtuse rubbish.

How can a triangle be cute?

Circumference of a circle drove me round the bend; I kept stabbing myself with the jaggy bit of the circle-drawing-pencil-holder-thing. And as for my scale drawings, well, they were astronomical! They were so good that the teacher held them up in front of the class as an example.

'And what's this one supposed to be, Miss Calderwood?'

'It's a parla-parla-parla-lell...'

He had to ask, didn't he.

The whole class was in eruptions. It was worse than a chimps' tea party.

'Parla-parla-parla-lerlo-gram!'

HAHAHA OO OO OO

The monkeys rocked back and forth in their seats, slapping the desks and each other with their jungle-green jotters.

Shapes are rubbish. I hate Maths.

Then the maths teacher gave us equations:

$a + b = c, x + y = z$

And all that jazz.

This is great, adding letters! 'Calderwood!' shouted monkey man, from up the back. 'What you writing?' This was *the duff class* (exclusively for head cases, dyslexics and dunces) and anyone who actually did any work was considered weird. I had a double page spread of as and bs and brackets.

I liked equations. I didn't know what a variable was or even why we were doing the funny alphabet sums but it was better than stupid shapes, any day. I liked putting curls on the legs of the xs, just like they did in the textbooks. I liked the wiggly brackets as well: {!}

'Hey, Calderwood! What did you get for 1 D?'

'2ab.'

'Howzat Frank Einstein? I thought a's and b's couldn't get added together?'

Fifty-eight per cent – top of the class for the algebra test. I didn't stay in the duff class for long. A few days later, I was moved up to the *reasonably stupid class*.

Then there was the Language Department. It was humiliating enough to be hauled in front of a whole class to recite French but did the teacher really have to chant out my downtrodden grade, as well?

The big-eared, long-faced donkey boy sitting in front of me was swinging on his chair and nudging my pencil case onto the floor.

'Merde!' shouted Jackass.

The yobs laughed like a pack of hyenas on helium.

'Shyay voodress oon hot dog a la merde!' he brayed. The teacher looked on in silence. 'Calderwood a la merde!' barked someone else.

He's right. My work is shit. I always get the worst marks.

I hated French.

Je deteste le française. Or is it la français? What is it with the la la la rubbish anyway?

I'd been plonked into a third-year mixed ability French class and I was expected to pick up what everyone else had been learning for the last two and a half years overnight. I could barely comprehend 'noun' or 'adjective' in basic English grammar. They might as well have been trying to teach me Punjabi for all the difference it would have made.

I could put on a great French accent, though. That's how I managed to wangle the part of the French teacher at Youth Theatre.

'Bonjour, la classe. Quelle est le date ton au jourd'hui?' I could do an excellent impression of our French teacher. This is the longest French phrase I can remember by heart – And even then I'm not sure of the spelling.

So when it came to the French speaking tests, I didn't do as badly because I could mimic the phonetics. My perfect accent scored me extra points. We were allowed to practise our 'conversations' quietly, with a friend, right up until it was our turn to speak. I managed to retain the sounds and syllables in my head, long enough to churn out cabalistic replies. It didn't matter what it meant. My first priority was making it sound the way the teacher wanted to hear it. And it worked for a while. Right up until the day she asked me, what kind of film I wanted to see at the cinema. I replied, in perfect French,

'A hot dog with tomato sauce.'

She made me repeat it for the class. They howled with laughter and I sat, ashen-faced, completely oblivious to my blunder. It was only after class that someone told me: I'd parroted the answer to the next question.

And then I had to contend with German too. But there was a difference – it was German for beginners. I was allowed to ask questions, I could afford to make mistakes. It was easier. Because I started from the beginning. A little easier because no one else in the class knew any German.

'Well, you'll have a bit of an advantage,' said the German teacher, 'You started this class, last year, didn't you?'

Here we go again with the memory thing. Why do I bother at all?

'Lucky if she ends up stacking shelves in Safeway,' was the Guidance teacher's contribution to my parents' interview.

The parents had been summoned to the school after a teacher had highlighted the slump in my grades from ninety-eight per cent to two per cent. One teacher. One teacher realized there was something wrong. It turned out that his wife had had a brain injury too. The rest had all put it down to 'laziness'. I was supposed to be receiving learning support. The Guidance teacher had all the medical reports. By this time, my parents were starting to realize that talking to her was about as effective as hitting my head against a brick wall!

'We think it would be better if you repeated a year.'

'We think it would be better if you repeated a year.'

'We think it would be better if you repeated a year.'

The school, the hospital, the parents: they all thought it would be better if I repeated a year.

I don't want to repeat anything she's done.

'Oh, you'll be in my year,' said Tracy.

Mmm, maybe it won't be so bad.

'Hey, memory woman! How come you got kept back a year?'

Kept back! Kept back!

I didn't like that phrase, 'kept back'. It was bad enough saying I was 'repeating' a year but 'kept back' – That was like saying I was backwards.

Nobody kept me back, it was my decision.

It was the first decision I had made for myself since the accident and, even then, I felt like I was being pushed.

'I'm repeating a year,' I'd tell them, matter-of-factly.

'Oooh, repeating a year!'

'I heard you used to be brainy?' wheedled one of the uniform yobs.

'–Yeah, what happened to you?'

Used to be. Used to be. Why can't I be the way I used to be?

I repeated the third year to catch up on the work I had missed.

Umm, I can't even remember the work I've supposed to have done.

I'm going to do my homework at my friend's house. I can't remember her name but she's my friend from the new maths class. She wants me to show her how to do equations.

It's 8:30pm. (I got a digital watch because I kept wearing the other one upside down and I couldn't tell the time when the hands were always back to front.) It's not dark but I don't like walking around at night. A sinister crowd of Adidas tracksuit yobs are kicking the shit out of a leather football in the street. I recognize some of them as idiots from school. A dizzy red-head girl with eyes like flying saucers shouts something at me, which I don't hear.

'Sorry?' I reply.

'You will be,' she snarls.

I've no idea what I've supposed to have done.

Did I hurt her in another life?

It's hard to tell sometimes, when you hear the stories from people who apparently, know me, her, it, the thing, the other one of me. It's hard to differentiate between the factual, the semi-fictional and the far out fairy tales.

'I can't believe you don't remember your first kiss...'

'Hey, do you remember you used to go with that guy...'

'Remember that time you got shagged...'

WHA-AAT?

'I remember that as well, it was the round the back of the...'

'No I didn't. You're a liar.'

'That's not very nice. We're just trying to help.'

'Yeah, I thought you couldn't remember anything?'

The dizzy red-head is two years younger than me and a trouble-maker. I've never spoken to her before (to my knowledge) but I've seen her in the school dinner hall, pushing people and skipping the queue. Her brother swaggers over towards us, crushing the ball to his chest. He is slightly older and much taller than me. I've never seen him before but I know that they are brother and sister as they have the same offensive orange hair and crazy psychedelic eyes.

'She was staring at me, drawing me dirty looks,' lied the dizzy red-head.

I was not. Liar.

'Yeah, she did. I saw her,' smirked a roly-poly girl with a face like Humpty Dumpty.

'Were you annoying my sister?' growled the crazy-eyed-boy.

We kept walking, trying to ignore them.

The dizzy red-head raised her voice,'Do you remember that freak I told you about, the one that lost her memory? That's her. She's a freak!'

I wanted to shrivel up and die. Every bleary eyeball on the street was on me. 'Shut it,' piped up my friend, 'Just ignore them,' she grabbed my arm, steering me past the baying crowd. They continued to follow us. Chanting:

FREAK-A-FREAK-A- FREAK-A-FREAK-A-FREAKFREAKFREAK

'Hey freak,' squinted the dizzy red-head, 'do you remember how to fight?' She skipped in front of us, blocking our path, arms folded tight across her skinny chest.

'I don't want to fight you, just leave me alone,' I muttered.

'No, I don't think you do want to fight her,' the crazy-eyed boy stepped in, 'You're too old for her. I'll fight you instead.'

'Look, I don't...'

CRUNCH.

A hard round fist slams harshly into the side of my head.

Ugh. What? Sorehead. Diz-zy. Where me? What?

I slump against the orange brick wall trying to steady myself.

I can't focus. Whoever said that you see stars when you are dazed was wrong – I can see black and white checkered squares.

Now it's going fuzzy.

↑⇨↙↙↕⏋ ⇨⇨△◀↑ ⇨⇨↙↙↓↔→ ∩◢↔▽⇨◢⏋

I sit down on the kerb to stop myself from falling.

'You fucking idiot,' my what-do-you-call-it – umm – my friend is screaming, 'she's had a head injury!'

'I think he's knocked her out,' panics the dizzy red-head.

'Yeah, you fucking idiot,' repeats Miss Dumpty, 'What did you do that for?'

'Yeah,' says Dizzy, what did you do that for?'

'Don't fucking look at me–'

The voices are swimming, echoing, hard and soft in my ears.

I wish they'd all just be quiet.

'Is she going to lose her memory?'

⇉▽ ▽↑⇨ →↕↓↔→ ◀↕ ↙↕▽⇨ ↑⇨△ ↘⇨↘↕△◢◤

The buildings are swaying and waving like flags.

Who said that? No, no, not again.

I let out a whimper and try to stand up.

↱↑⇨◀ ↓▽ →↕↓↔→ ↕↔↲

'I'm going to get my mum from the pub,' rambles Miss Dumpty.

'I'm going home,' mutters the crazy-eyed boy, 'I'm not getting the fucking blame for this.'

```
The       wor      ld
is
S    low    ly
com              ing
back     in     to      fo     cus.
```

The crazy-eyed-boy is running up the road like a bat out of hell and the concerned parent is staring into my eyes.

'Drunk. She's drunk.'

'No, she's not,' snapped my friend. 'He punched her.'

'I'll boot that boy's arse if I get him,' she says.

'Hey is that the wee girl that lost her memory?'

'Yeah, do you think we should call an ambulance?'

'No, I'm fine.'

'See,' says the concerned parent, 'Maybe that bang on the head has done her the world of good.'

What?

'You see that happening all the time on the telly,' she dribbles, 'folk getting their memory back.'

I sobbed all the way home. I felt so hollow. How could people be so malicious?

I am never going back to that school. I've worked so hard; I've tried so hard.

Remember me freak?

Memory woman go back to your own time zone

and

Alien everyone hates you go back to your own planet

These were just some of the anonymous notes I received. Whoever they were, they were such cowards that they couldn't even sign their name and had to use stencils.

Social integration was especially difficult because my disability was hidden. I never wanted sympathy but I could have done without the added pressure of hostility. I also resented being grouped into a social category with other sufferers. I didn't want to be allocated the description 'disabled' or 'brain damaged' or 'subnormal intelligence' (the latter is often coupled with brain injury stigmata). I wanted people to accept that I had a head injury but I also wanted to distinguish myself from their vague speculations about the stereotypical brain injury sufferer.

When I found out I was to go to a new school two towns away, I felt like turning cartwheels. I thought I'd be able to start over, devise my own identity. No one at the new school would know me. No one at the new school would remember the other Lynsey.

Chapter 6

New School + New Friends

I hover, nervously, outside the big classroom. Inside the hordes are intimidating. I'm told that two guidance classes have been squashed together to make one ginormous class and they are supposed to be watching a video about careers.

PSSST WSSSAWSSSA WSSSA

I can hear them whispering and giggling.

> I know they are all talking about me. I chisel nervously at the edges of my crinkle cut nails.

A booming voice hollers for me to enter. My guidance teacher, Mr Gorilla-pits, is a short, balding man in his fifties with patches of greasy silver hair and a large paunch. His sleeves are rolled up to his elbows revealing his furry King Kong arms and there are visible sweat patches around the armpits of his blue shirt. 'This is the new kid,' he announces. I cringe as he puts one pudgy hand lightly, on my shoulder and tells me to 'park my butt' in a seat.

I am marooned next to an itchy-looking, spot-picking monkey-boy who appears to have a compulsion to continually claw at his head.

PSSST PSSST WSSSA WSSSA

'Oh look, the new girl's got a new boyfriend!'

I pretend not to hear but I can feel the contours of my face burn deep crimson. Itchy doesn't seem to mind, he just grins vaguely, mutters to himself and proceeds to scratch his head.

I try to avoid making eye contact with anyone, but a slim, earnest looking boy with a smooth alabaster complexion catches my eye, peering out at me from behind his soft, shiny blonde hair. Transfixed by his gaze, I don't know whether to smile or look away. A month later, the same boy sent me my first ever Valentine card.

Gorilla-pits has volunteered a girl with a hard-to-pronounce name to guide me around the school. My head is spinning with all the whatsits and whodunits that are being hurled at me. Funny-name girl introduces to me to several people including thingummy, him-with-the-hair and whatserface.

I just want everyone to like me. I want to please everyone by answering their questions but I am wary of them finding too much out about my past. I don't want to be known as a freak or the 'memory woman'. I just want to make friends and get on with my life.

I feel so insecure, sitting in a gargantuan classroom with strangers eyeballing me like some kind of new specimen, zooming in on my every move, my every error. I am far away from home and my parents. I don't know these strange people.

BUT...

They don't know me either.

They don't know about my brain injury.

They don't know the other Lynsey.

What if I get lost and everyone laughs at me? What if I forget people's names and conversations I've had?

I was a bit of an enigma. I had joined the new school a month after the Christmas holidays in the middle of a standard grade year.

PSSST...WSSSA WSSSA WSSSA WSSSA

'What made you leave halfway through fourth year?' asked Regatta-jacket-number-one.

'Yeah,' said Regatta-jacket-number-two, 'what made you come to this school?'

'Two buses away,' chipped in Regatta-jacket-number-three.

It was rumoured that I had been expelled from my last school.

'Whereabouts is it you stay?'

'Umm, Renfrew.'

'My cousin stays in Renfrew,' says Regatta-jacket-number-three. 'Do you know –'

'I don't know anyone.'

Shit, I hope she doesn't ask her cousin if she knows me.

Finally, the excitement has died down. This is the hard part now. Explaining how I am still getting lost and forgetting things even though I've been at the school for almost six weeks. And trying to remember everyone's name is a nightmare. I have even started to make notes on who was in all the different classes with me. The hardest thing is finding my way round the school and remembering where all the different classes are. I am petrified I will get lost and show myself up. I make a list of who sits next to me in what class.

Lynsey sits to the left of me in maths.
One of the Garys sits to the right of me in Art.
The girl who always eats a Twix sits to the left of me in the other Art class.
Lynsey and the two Donnas sit at my group for RE.

I hope Lynsey is never off sick because she's in most of my classes.

As long as I know what class I have next, I can always make sure I am standing beside someone in that class when the bell rings.

My doubts keep mounting up.

I really want to finish school but I don't know if I can cope. The work is hard and exams are looming. People keep asking me why I don't have a full timetable. How do I communicate to teachers that I need extra help without looking like some kind of numskull?

I feel like an inadequate sub-specimen. I'm taking only four standard grades as opposed to everyone else's eight. I can't let them find out that I was too thick to cope with a full timetable at the other school. That would be so mortifying.

I stick rigidly to my story that the curriculum here is different and that's why I've had to abort four subjects. I don't want anyone thinking that I'm intellectually challenged. Anyway, they'll have to believe me about the German class because they don't do German at this school.

Lynsey. Another Lynsey. Blue eyes, wavy brown hair, just like me. She likes Take That; Robbie Williams is her favourite too!

'How do you spell your name?' I ask, suspiciously.

'L–Y–N–S–E–Y.'

'Me too!'

Maybe I could transform into Lynsey M instead of Lynsey C. We soon became inseparable. School lives, loves lives, home lives entwined. At school everyone referred to us as 'The Lynseys', said we were like twins. It didn't matter that there was an eleven-month age gap or a six-inch deficit in height. We were joined at the brain. We'd finish each other's sentences, link arms and do 'the wacky walk' and drive our classmates and our boyfriends mad with the 'twinnie' thing.

'I stayed up to watch *Prisoner: Cell Block H* last night,'

'Twinnies!'

'I bought the new *Take That* single at the weekend,'

'Twinnies!'

'Remix 1&2.'

'Twinnies!!!' We'd lock pinkies, smile and squeal 'Twinnies' in unison: the sacred symbol of our 'twinliness'.

It didn't really bother us when the teachers separated us for our mischief. We'd just spend more time passing notes and inventing new methods of communication, paper aeroplanes, coded messages written on the backs of rubbers and rulers. We believed our friendship was unbreakable, impermeable and everlasting. It never occurred to us that at some point we'd have to establish our own identity and make grown up decisions on our own.

Years later, Lynsey and I – so very different and established in our own personas – we laugh about 'the twin thing' and can't even remember what it was that shelved our friendship for almost four years.

For me, I think the last straw was when she copied my handwriting. My handwriting of many twirls and curls, with it's little 'x's above the 'i's. I even learnt mirror writing so well that I can write as elegantly in reverse as I can in the regular fashion. 'But that just shows how silly I was,' she told me recently, 'I thought I was being flattering.'

I still remember her last words to me when I left that school:

'You're better than the whole damn lot of them put together,' she told me. By 'them' she meant the rest of the kids in our year and the teachers who were about to fail me yet again. Even though we'd hardly spoken for the past year, I could still sense that she cared.

They've given me a special needs teacher. She's nice. Special keyboarding skills because it takes me t...e...n m...i...l...l...i-...o...n y...e...a...r...s... to write things down. The only time she can teach me, though, is during one block of my History classes so I have to get a 'timetable change'.

The learning support department has promised me that when I learn to type, the school will supply a laptop so that I can manage my work. It's hard at first, learning to find all the letter buttons, and sometimes I just want to punch the screen till its RAMchips all fizzle and fry and it all blows up like a rocket to the moon. The computer squeals every time I make a mistake.

Once upon a time

Once upone —**bleep** s —**bleep** a

Once a —**bleep** upon a time

U —bleep nce upon a time

It's really embarrassing when that thing bleeps. The Office Information Studies class is on at the same time as my keyboard skills class and I have to sit at the back of the class. Most people are snapping at their keyboards with two-fingered punches but I really want to learn to type. I want to learn to type so that I can type a whole book.

A bottle-blonde gremlin girl growls at me. I can't help but stare at her atrocious ginger roots.

She's one of the ugliest people I have ever seen in my life. Her hair looks like straw hanging out of a bin.

'You're wasting your time,' she sneers, 'No one ever learns to type in this class. Why don't you just use two fingers like everyone else.'

I feel like giving you a two-fingered salute.

I just ignore her and keep on typing because I want that little carry-around computer and I want to write that book.

Getting out of class for my own private lesson – I didn't resent this. I loved being different most of the time. I liked being able to work on my own in the library because I couldn't concentrate when other people talked in the class. Some of my friends were jealous. I knew I was different and they knew there was something different about me. I didn't tell them I had a disability, though. Later on, as my insecurities developed with my body, I was not so comfortable with being different. In school, teachers had to know about my brain injury so they wouldn't expect me to perform the work at the same pace as everyone else.

I am really lonely. I can't join in all the conversations that everyone else has because I am never in class. Somebody in school today said to me, 'You are so lucky to have free periods.' Free periods to catch up on work I've missed. Free periods to catch up on work I haven't missed. Free periods to sort my bag out. Free periods to work out exactly where I've lost my jotter and how many pencils I've accidentally stolen.

I have acquired another miscellaneous item of stationery: a limp black pen with no lid. I've no idea where I got it from.

It's not mine – someone has chewed the end – that's not my brand of bite mark.

At school I used my power of memory loss selectively, it seemed. Library books would accumulate inside my bookcase at home and in my locker at school. I once totted up seven copies of *The Great Gatsby* (one of my favourite books). I studied it for Higher English: 'Chapter 5 is the pivotal chapter of *The Great Gatsby*...the main plot moves inexorably toward the crisis in Chapter 7 that leads to Gatsby's death in Chapter 8...main theme surrounding Gatsby...'

EH?

In the third year, I had systematically worked my way through the fifth and sixth year higher reading list. I enjoyed swallowing books that confuddled my friends, but some parts of my brain just didn't seem to compute. I understood what I read as I was reading it but, each time I finished a chapter, I couldn't remember the details. I'd stop for a five-minute break and I'd have to retrace the pages I'd just read. I loved English but I constantly fell behind in class as I struggled to remember the names of characters, and what happened in which story.

'Who can tell me about Daisy Buchanan's role?'

EH?

I'd read the book seven times so far. Seven was my favourite lucky number. I thought it might bring me luck, I might remember it better if I read it seven times over. I went a bit 'seven-crazy' for a while. Everything had to be number seven: seven steps up the stairs, seven walks across the road, and seven spreads to spread the margarine on my bread.

It says it in one of my books: 7 is a magic number.

7-7-7-7-7 7-7
DAT-DA-DA-DA-DAH. DAT-DAT.
She tapped on her desk with the lid of her pen. My head shot up and my eyes locked on hers.

Heebie-jeebie, man. Shit, how did she know to knock seven times?

'Lynsey, why do you think Daisy stayed with Tom?'

Tom-Tom Tom-Tom-Tom. Who's Tom?

'Did you like Daisy as a character?'

'Uh… Gatsby went to great lengths to achieve wealth to lure Daisy back.'

'Yes, but that's not what I asked,' she said, gawking at me over her silver-rimmed spectacles, obviously awaiting some alluring answer that she wasn't going to get from me. She could have been saying 'the cat sat on the mat' but I was translating it as 'one flew over the cuckoo's nest'. But it wasn't just English teacher number six, it was every teacher, in every class.

I still possess a reference book from the school library, about animals in captivity

How embarrassing, there is no way that I am handing that back now.

Recently, I came across a hoard of books that I had borrowed from my sister, which she had actually borrowed from her school library, last year.

OH DEAR. I wonder if she wants them back?!?

Generally, the public library is good at chasing me up. I always try to respond immediately to their letters regarding overdue books, apologizing profoundly for their lateness and humbly paying the respective fines. I am addicted to buying discard books from the library. There seems to be something spiritual about second-hand books. The worn pages give them character and I believe there is some variant of karma that passes emotions and intelligence from one reader to the next. The same applies to possessions, although I will not buy second-hand clothes because I would rather not walk 'in someone else's shoes'. Perhaps these feelings stem from a time when I was resigned to wearing clothes I did not remember choosing.

Fragments of the Past

Mirror, Mirror
On the floor
Lie shattered pieces
Of my life.

My reflection
Hosts so many strange faces
Lost in the loneliness;
I feel part of another species.

I dress myself up
And dust myself down;
I wipe the smile
Clean off my face

Then, I hide
In the closet
With open wounds
Undressed.

'Someone keeps stealing my socks!'

'Who would steal your socks, Lynsey?'

'I don't know,' I whine, 'A sock stealer.'

'Don't be so childish. Look for them.'

'Can't.'

'Well, maybe if you took your socks off and placed them properly in the washing basket instead of leaving them tucked inside your trouser legs then they wouldn't get lost,' concludes my mother as she rummages through the washing basket.

I stopped wearing socks. I would walk around barefoot, regardless of blisters with the laces of my Caterpillar boots spilling out like spaghetti strands. My mother thought it was a teenage thing.

'Tie those laces,' she'd say to me, 'I can't understand why you don't wear socks.'

'Nobody wears socks,' I rolled my eyes, 'and I'll look sad if I tie my laces.'

Cold Feet

To die in a
White darkness is
Close to flying
Blindfolded with
Glasses. It's rude
To stare at blue

Cheese and silly
To sneeze at a
Butterfly (I'd
Just like to smell
The brightness of
His wings). I'd like

To fall into
Softness and just
Disappear through
A silent ring
Of darkness. In
Time, I'll wear socks.

Truth was, I couldn't tie a bow and socks were just another task for me to struggle with in the morning.

At least at the adolescent unit they let us wear slippers.

Off with the shoes! As soon as I fly through the front door, the bag, the jacket, the shoes are kicked into different directions.
'Who's in the toilet?'
No answer.

BANG-A-BANG-A-BANG-A-THUDDD

'HURRY UP!'

The toilet flushes and the door unlocks. I nearly bowl the sister over. 'Keep your knickers on,' she smirks.

SLAM.

I am accosted as I try to make a sharp exit from the bathroom.

'Lynsey,' scolds the mother, 'shoes and bags *do not* belong in the hall.' The mother hovers over me as I treasure hunt for the keys that have escaped from my bag, mid-flight.

'Well,' I said, 'I was needing in.'

The keys are not there. Somebody must have moved them.

STOMP-A-STOMP-A-STOMP-A-STOMPPP

'Lynsey, stop that banging, right now.'

Nag-fucking-nag

'I can't find my keys.'

'Have you looked?'

HMMMPHHUMMPHHURRUMMPHH

I scrutinize the pinholes on the carpet.

'Not here,' I sing, triumphantly. 'Somebody's done something with them.'

The mother thumps into the hall.

'Lynsey,' she says, 'how many times do I have to say that there are no thieves in this house.'

In between all the kerfuffle, the sister has just bungee-jumped into the hall, picked up my keys from the phone table and is swinging them under our noses.

'Well, somebody must've moved them.'

'I put them there because they were lying on the floor,' says the sister, smugly.

See, stealing my stuff. Trying to trick me.

'That's what happens,' says the mother, resolutely, 'when you leave everything at your backside.'

HUMPH.

I slam into my room.

'Lynsey,' shouts the moaning mother.

Oh, what now?

'Here's your keys.'

I developed an 'attitude problem'. That's what the parents said, anyway.

My friends often teased me indirectly about my forgetfulness. In school, I shrugged their comments off but when I returned home, my anger would erupt if I couldn't get everything 100 per cent my own way. I took my frustration out on my family whose elastoplast tolerance had been stretched much further than my friends. I also enjoyed attacking inanimate objects because they couldn't argue back.

ॐ

I was having a good dream – I can't remember what – But it wasn't the usual kind of dream where my teeth fall out or the Vampire bleeds from her eyes. I think there might have been some kind of siren in the dream, I'm not sure because the mother came in and ruined it all.

'Get up!' She snapped. 'You'll be late for school.'

Who cares?

I wanted to cling onto sleep and finish the ending of my dream. It was like watching a TV programme when someone comes in and starts talking and you miss all the good bits.

'Are you deaf?'

Eh? Yes.

'It's quarter to eight,' she said, scraping the covers off my back, with the dream being sucked into extinction almost as if she had switched the TV off by remote control. I thump out of bed, crunching my heel on something cold and hard. Grimacing in pain, I look down to find my alarm clock lying on its side with its brains hanging out.

And there was nothing decent to eat either. I wanted a nice happy red apple to munch on the way to school but all that was left was a gang of sickly looking green apples congregating in the fruit bowl like a bunch of old women. I hate rotten green apples with their sour taste and hard skin; they crunch like old decrepit bones when you bite into them.

I need a cigarette to cure my hunger. I have to wait until I'm out of my street in case some nosy person sees me and tells the mother.

CLICK-A-CLICK-A-CLICK-A-CLICK-A-CLIKKK

My lighter isn't even working. It's one of those three for a pound ones that I got from a street vendor. Someone has stolen the good one with the green and orange stripes that I got from Tesco.

There's a scrawny bloodless green granny hunched over by the side of the kerb. I suppose I should help her to cross the road.

Here you go, Granny–

KER-RACK!

Wow, look at her go! I gave her a right good kick up the backside

I watch the fusty old fruit spewing brown mucous from a bruise on her left temple as she scuds across the road and straight under the wheels of a passing car. Her skeleton crumbles to a skinny watery pulp and I catch myself from laughing, satanically, just in time to witness the car skid and screech to a halt, a few feet short of a garden gate.

SHIT!

I sprint across the road. Down the lane and all the way to school. I run like a dog, the hood of my jacket flapping like a huge velvet ear. I pray that no one had seen me. And all because of an apple…

Oh, how I hate you rotten green apples.

I didn't mean it. It just happened.

It was a bit like that time when I accidentally shoplifted the loaf of bread. I was in the supermarket with the mother and she was letting me push the trolley.

I'm good at this.

WHEEEEEEEEEEEEEEEEEEEEEEEEEEEEEEEEEEEEEECLUNK

'Lynsey!' The mother growled at me and stopped to take her shoe off. 'You went right up my heels there.'

SIGH.

'Right,' she said. 'I'll take the trolley and you can go and get me a loaf.'

I dawdled around the aisles, round and round until I got to the bread bit. When I got back, she'd begun to stack the messages onto the rolling counter. I watched the long-nosed, bleary-eyed check out operator roll the scanner thing over our groceries.

BLEEP-BLEEP-BLEEEEP

The macaroni wasn't scanning. It was the cheap disgusting cheesy-just-put-it-in-the-pot-and-add-milk-pasta.

That stuff tastes like worms. Well, it probably tastes worse than worms. In fact, it probably tastes like maggots.

I watched Long-nose turn the packet over and over as he tried again and again. 'It won't scan,' he said.

I don't know why you're looking at me. I don't know how to work it.

Eventually, someone came to his rescue and we got our macaroni.

We got the bus to the end of our road and then walked the rest of the way. It was the mother who spotted it. 'Lynsey,' she gasped, 'You didn't pay for that!'

There I was, still swinging the loaf in its plastic jacket. 'We'll need to take it back,' I panicked, 'to pay for it.'

'That will be right,' she snapped. 'My feet are killing me and it'll cost twice as much on the bus fare.'

Recently I was out for a pub lunch and on the way home, I realized that I had a copy of the menu in my bag.

I must've lifted it when I put my purse back.

It happens all the time, I'm an accidental shoplifter. It makes for interesting conversation.

Nowadays, I don't try to hide the fact that I have memory problems. Sometimes, it does annoy me, though, that seven years later, it is necessary for me to tick an extra little box and give lengthy explanations about my imperfections. The reactions on the whole are not so bad now. Occasionally, you get people who just don't want to understand and I must constantly explain, 'No, I am not lazy, I simply do not have the stamina nor the capability to go to work yet.' Besides, that is my prerogative. If people don't know about my disability and I have to do something which requires them knowing, I don't allow myself to worry about their reaction.

Hidden Disability

A little old lady swifter than me,
Swiveled past me with her walking stick and
Captured the last seat on the bus. 'Privilege
Seats for the elderly and disabled,'
She crowed, quoting from the bright white placard.
Staggering slightly; I cling on tightly
To the hand rail like an elastoplast,
Open my mouth to protest but then on
Second thoughts, say nothing. After all, who'd
Listen? I look just like everyone else.

It annoys me when pensioners tell me not to sit at the front of the bus or when bus drivers snatch away my bus card:

I boarded the bus with the sister and showed my card.

'Which one of you is disabled?' he sneered. He didn't give me a chance to say anything before he added, 'I mean, you look fine to me. Nothing wrong with you.'

Gobsmacked, I replied, 'It's a hidden disability, actually.'

If I need help with something, I'll ask. If I get lost, I'll ask for directions. I'll make jokes about the situations I get into when I am lost, ending up in the gents toilets (which could happen to anyone) or traveling about 100 million miles in the wrong direction when I got on the Gourock train instead of Glasgow.

A blur of trees and red roofs whizzed past the window and all the time I was digging my nails into the red and black chequered fabric on the bus seat and biting a hole in my lip.

Where will this bus stop? I must have got the motorway bus by mistake.

The education authorities had given me a bus pass. However, at least twice a week I would get off at the wrong stop or get on the wrong bus. The last straw was when I walked six miles home in the snow along a country road. When the mother asked how I managed to find my way home, I simply said, 'There were buses coming towards me and buses in front of me so I just picked a bus and followed it until I came to our bus stop.' From that moment on, I was issued a taxi.

I think I definitely underestimated my new friends by expecting some big reaction. They weren't like the kids from my old school; they didn't known what I was like before and so they couldn't make comparisons or assumptions. Everyone had their own things to deal with which didn't leave much time for thinking about me and my disability twenty-four hours a day. But at the time, my mind was consumed with dread and paranoia as I tried to live my life under-cover. Dealing with my anxiety was harder than dealing with the outcome of my brain injury. My life was different from most other teenagers. It meant missing a lot of school for doctors' appointments and I found it increasingly difficult to keep up with everyone else and to conceal my disability.

I am standing in the dinner queue. I'm trying to think. A crusty-fusty-faced dinner woman is rushing me. I don't know what to choose: the chips are black. There's no baked potatoes left and I've never tried any of the other foods: big gigantic crispy things called poppadoms; some kind of browny-red-grey foreign muck with big purple and black bits of raisins in it.

I'm getting tremors in my left hand and
I can feel my tray tilting from side to side
I drop
    my knife
        and fork
My hand won't stop shaking.

Funny-name girl picks up my cutlery. I try to laugh it off.

'That used to happen to my mum,' said funny-name girl. 'She had a trapped nerve in her hand.'

I nod, grasp a plate of limp salad with both hands and shuffle over to the check out. We sit at our usual table and everyone is quiet. No one talks about it again until the day we are in the pool hall and I keep dropping the cue.

'What's up with your hand,' someone asks.

'Oh, I think it's a trapped nerve.'

School was so important to me – it was my life. I had, and still have an obsession with being intelligent. It didn't matter that I hadn't even decided what to do with my life, I just couldn't handle appearing stupid. I was trying to compete with my former self. I wanted to outshine her, prove that I could stretch my limits further:

> I cannot cope with feeling stupid. Having a crippled memory. No future, no life worth living. If I don't go to college it means no job. Not a decent job. What would the other Lynsey have been? A writer? Something intellectual. She would've wanted to go to uni, I bet. I've got to be better than her at something…

I set incredibly high standards for myself, and I refused to accept that I could not meet them. I finally had to admit that I had trouble learning French, not to mention biology (too much scientific jargon), and that it didn't really matter because I had no interest in pursuing either in college. At the time, I was annoyed. I had no confidence in myself. I saw this only as another failure.

I had five projects due in two weeks and wasn't coping with the work. Every day I woke up hating school and every night I went to sleep hating school. Academically, I had met all my deadlines so far but I'd no time left to do anything other than sleep.

> I've been trying very hard. Maybe everything will finally get better? I really feel that I am doing much better than last year but I still feel that I should be doing much more. I'm so scared of failing my classes. I'm sure things will never be perfect for me.

At the end of fourth year, the deputy head teacher gave me the Special Achievement Award. I resented it. I had barely said 'hello' to her all year.

> She doesn't know anything about me. Huh, she only got a file from the hospital detailing my differences, my disabilities.

I felt like she was rewarding me for my courage to try and be normal, a thing that is demanded of other students. I lost all respect for her then: she was insulting my intelligence and my self-esteem. I didn't need anyone to humour me like that. Even at sixteen, I was above that. I really began to distrust teachers after that, and distrust all compliments they gave me. It was a different world, at the second school. For the first time, boys began to ask me out. I was definitely afraid of them. None of them knew about my disability and I didn't want to bring up the topic. I was terrified of their reaction. I began hiding my personality out of insecurity. I felt I couldn't express my humour, opinions – anything. My life was a paradox because I was not in touch with myself yet I had no concept of a reality existing outside of me. My world was filled with gossip and empty friendships. It was all so superficial. I just tried to pretend I felt like I fitted in.

Chapter 7

Anorexia, the Gym
+ Exercise Addiction

Sometimes, I feel like I am being robbed of my disease. I want to hold onto my precious symptoms of anorexia. I might want to use them again, if the need arises.

When people ask me questions like:

Why did I want to lose weight in the first place?

Did I choose to have an eating disorder?

What do I think *made* me become anorexic?

I simply tell them, 'Sometimes it's easier being ill. When you have anorexia you only have one big problem eating at you.'

My eating disorders had been constant companions since my brain injury. They had been my most faithful allies and worst adversaries. I found comfort in my secret binges but was also dogged with guilt and shame from purging. I felt like I was crazy and the only one who did these disgusting things.

As the teenage years receded, I watched my beauty thicken. I felt as though I was being thrust into womanhood and my powers of decision making had been taken from me: parents, teachers, friends – they all expected me to conform to their images of what they thought I should be. So I did the only thing I could to express myself: I developed a strange and individual talent that I could control, expertly.

Head spinning, body tingling, and a strange sensation down my left side.

I have to hurry home.

The more I hurry, the more I worry, heart beating faster, can't breathe, legs go numb, think I'm going to die.

I can't control the way my brain works but I can control what I put in my body.

When I arrive home, the feeling has passed and I'm not scared anymore. Glad to be home. Lie in bed thinking about death and damnation and eternity.

'Too much stress, you worry too much,' people say to me.

I continue searching for answers and rediscover an effective form of self-medication: bingeing and purging. Surprised at how good it makes me feel. Successfully numbing the pain.

Soon it controlled me. I finally realized that it was called bulimia when I saw the film *Kate's Secret* on cable TV, a story about a housewife and perfect mother who binged in secret and made herself sick when she was depressed. I was watching the show with my parents and thinking to myself,

That's crazy, she's not fat. How can she be bulimic?

'That's disgusting,' commented my father while I sat cringing. 'Turn that off.'

No, I want to watch it. I want to see what happens to her.

My mother added, 'You wonder how that happens to folk?'

Then I began thinking about the anorexic girl.

Didn't she say she used to be bulimic? No, I'm not going to end up like her.

The tears were burning the backs of my eyeballs. How could I ever possibly tell anyone? They would think I was disgusting.

I feel like throwing up because that would make me feel better, and wouldn't feel disgusting anymore, but right now the parents are home, and I don't want them to find out.

So I began a quest. I wanted to know as much as I possibly could about bulimia. As I read, I was amazed. I thought I was learning something that would help me considerably. I became hyper-vigilant, collecting every article I could on the subject. I read all the self-help books. I wanted to purge myself of this disease. I was searching for some magical overnight cure but it didn't exist. Eventually, hunger would drive me to the kitchen but I'd feel overwhelmingly apprehensive.

Fruit Clubs are coming back to haunt me. Suddenly the mother has been buying them in abundance. Our fridge is choc-full of the smarmy little bastards in their silver shell suits and snug purple jackets, peering at me from behind the Mars Bars.

I think about what to eat as soon as I get up.

Am I really this hungry?

Toast, more toast, a litre of milk, handfuls of dry cereal from the packet. Filling the hole of an empty day.

I was horrified when the mother said I had 'good sturdy legs.' The very idea of being sturdy repulsed me. The word tasted like bile in my mouth:

I am a size twelve, I am ugly and I have horrible hair and oh – Let's not forget that I puke every day. I want to be a size six or eight. I

want to be thin, not 'sturdy'. I want to be the thinnest person in the world.

'I'm nine stone according to your Granny's scales,' said the father (everyone was nine stone according to those stupid scales). All the colour drained from my face when I heard him say this. There he was, a man in his forties, an inch taller than me.

He should be much much heavier.

He was admittedly underweight. I didn't see it like that though. I could only see it as an implication that I had a weight problem. At my heaviest, I was 8 stone 11, only three pounds lighter. I felt ashamed. Ashamed of our almost identical girth.

I'm not suggesting that my father's remark was a trigger for my anorexia (nor was there any malice intentionally directed at my weight), merely that the comments I heard were stored in the back corner of my mind and later retrieved to be used in evidence against my body.

For three years, I carefully concealed my bulimia from my friends and family. I was ashamed of my embarrassing 'habit' of bingeing and purging. I quickly got into a routine: wake up, have breakfast, throw up, go to school, have lunch, throw up, go home, have dinner, throw up, go to bed, wake up, binge, throw up, go back to bed.

When Life Eats In At You

Bottomless pit
Of despair. Couldn't care
If I live or die.
Pangs of hunger,
Pangs of guilt;

I've built
My life around my lies,
My secrets; I despise
The tasteless creature
I've become.

Every mouthful,
Every morsel;
Feeling so remorseful
Every time I take a bite
Of breath.

Starved of
Love and happiness;
I digest only the loneliness
That life dishes out
To me.

I supposed I was weak and disgusting and I was terrified of how my family would react if they ever discovered my secret. Guilt and isolation drove me deeply into depression. I scoured the libraries for self-help books, desperate for a solution, craving normality. It just didn't occur to me, at the time, that in my efforts to heal myself, I was serving myself up a whole new set of obsessions.

In the early throes of anorexia I was so eclipsed by euphoria and the flattering idea that I (alone) was curing myself that I hardly recognized how rapidly my preoccupation with body image and food was developing. Those first few pounds I shed did not go unnoticed.

'Hey, looking good, Lyns,' said the slim-athletic-popular girl, while eating a chewy-fatty-burger-van burger. 'Have you lost weight?'

Eugh, food poisoning, I'd never eat anything off the burger van.

'Thanks. Yeah, I've lost a bit.'

'I'm trying to put weight on.'

Bitch. Rub it in, why don't you.

'I've got another half a stone to lose.'

'What for? You look great.'

'Really? I didn't think anyone had noticed.'

'Yeah, your face looks really slim. Just don't lose too much weight.'

Yeah, whatever.

Elated, I received compliments in abundance and I revelled in the glory of becoming a size ten (the number was like some kind of status symbol). For the first time since my accident I was beginning to believe I could succeed at something. I felt invincible.

I liked secrets. When the stress of school and secrets and perfection overwhelmed me, I would comfort myself with crisps and chocolate. I remember watching the anorexic girl reject food in the adolescent unit, but it never occurred to me then to ask for help. I often wondered where she was and how things had turned out for her.

I wonder if she's alive or dead? If she still thinks about me? What would she say if she knew about me? I want to try and contact her but I'm so ashamed of what I am. I feel like I've let her down. Let everyone down.

When I saw other people struggling with their weight, I would watch and listen.

'I'm on a diet,' said the chicken-curry-and-chips-for-lunch-every-day-I'm-not-fat-I'm-just-big-boned Elephant-girl.

'Don't be daft,' said Junkfood-junkie girl, shovelling vinegary chips and chip-shop pickled onions, alternately, before tipping back her head and emptying an entire packet of Rubble bubble gum into her mouth. 'You're not fat.'

Aww, disgusting.

'I'm fifteen stone.'

Aww, disgusting.

'You're just –'

Heavy boned.

'heavy boned.'

Is she hell, she's an obese beast. I'd shoot myself if I got to that stage.

'Well, maybe I'll just have chicken curry with rice and a packet of crisps, instead of the chips.'

Oh, what an idiot. Does she know nothing at all about healthy eating? If I could swap bodies with her for a week, I bet I'd soon lose half her body weight.

I began to read newspapers regularly. I read about celebrities and their weight loss, it intrigued me. I would read personal stories by other anorexics, trying to convince myself that they were much worse than me and that I didn't have a problem.

What the scales said determined how I felt. Spending all my time focusing on calories meant that I didn't have time for anything else or anyone else – except Ed.

I've written a letter to my eating disorder. I don't know if this is weird or not, but I have always claimed it as mine, as a part of me, who I am. I am not entirely sure if that's healthy or normal, but I have a personal relationship and almost a respect for it. Sometimes it helps to write it all down when I feel this bad (Ed is the androgynous name I gave to that little voice that eats away at my self confidence).

Dear Ed,

Sometimes I wake up in the night so hungry that I wonder if it's all worth it. But when I step on the scales, I feel a little bit more worthwhile. Food is my every thought. I am my every thought. There is no room left for friends and family or schoolwork. There is only time for my eating disorder. You are the only one I can talk to. Everything revolves around my failures and achievements. How I punish myself or reward myself, how I push myself to try harder, how I have to work at losing weight. What will other people think of me if I put on weight? If I could just stay skinny, I would be happy forever. I always seem to be bordering on temporary insanity.

I cut out many foods then finally whole food groups.

Dear Ed,

We watched a video on food poisoning today. I am never eating beef again. I am never eating eggs again. They are full of fat anyway. No one understands. Everyone at school makes jokes about me eating prunes and they call me a 'health freak'. Someone said I'd 'turn into a vegetable'.

I read in a book that it takes seven years to complete the full process of body detoxification:

- demi-vegetarian   (no red meat)

- pescatarian   (no meat apart from sea food)

- ovo-lacto vegetarian   (no fish)

- lacto-vegetarian   (no eggs)

- vegan   (no dairy products)

- fruitarian   (no grains or vegetables)

- breatharian   (no food)

Pseudo-vegetarians infuriated me. The lack of consistency in their diet annoyed me (not that it was any of my business). I'm-a-vegetarian-but-I-eat-dolphin-friendly-tuna told me that she ate eight fudges one day because there was 'nothing else to eat in the shop'. She worked in a newsagents/grocers. Of course, no one appreciated my interference; they laughed at my attempts at 'healthy eating' and called me the 'resident dietician'.

'Prunes!' Junkfood-junkie guffawed, 'Calderwood, what you doing eating prunes? Prunes make you shite!'

I was thrilled when people began to comment on my newfound thinness; it cancelled out the comments they made about my strange eating habits. I went through a phase of buying chocolate Kinder surprise eggs in bulk, but only for the surprise toys.

'Do you want the chocolate from these,' I asked Chip-shop boy.

'Do you not want it?'

'No, I'm collecting the wee cute penguin figures.'

'How many of them did you buy?'

'Ten. Here, this chocolate's stinking,' I said, extracting the plastic yellow egg from inside the brown and white chocolatey egg, 'I hate white chocolate.'

I loved the attention. I loved people telling me I'd lost weight and I took an excessive interest in the shape and size of others and what they ate. I cooked elaborately, criticized others' attempts to eat healthily or lose weight. I would become anxious and annoyed if anyone appeared to be thinner than me.

The skinny girl from drama was my friend but I was jealous of her lean frame and high angular cheekbones. (I couldn't believe it when I discovered three years later that she had also fallen victim to bulimia.)

I couldn't concentrate on schoolwork: I was too busy studying *Rosemary Conley's Hip and Thigh Diet Book* to be bothered about insignificant things like exams.

It's not like I'm going to pass anyway. Everyone's filling in their UCAS forms for university except me. I'm so stupid, I probably wouldn't get past the part where you fill in your name and address.

I'm scared of mirrors… *I am very scared of mirrors:*

In the mornings when I get up sometimes I just don't want to see my face. I'm ashamed of what I see: parchment thin skin, baggy eyes, swollen glands that make me look like a hamster.

The mother accosted me on my way to school this morning and told me I looked terrible.

I know, I'm so fat.

I've been really sick the past few days,

I don't know why.

I haven't even been throwing up,
but my muscles are aching
and my whole body feels weak
and I feel so nauseous
that it's practically impossible to even drink soup
because I feel so bloated.
Abdominal pains,
    blisters in my mouth,
feel like I've swallowed a packet of razors,
    throat hurts and itches,
can hardly talk.
I'm
really
really
tired
but it's 'probably just the flu'.

❧

I knew someone had told. I knew right away when the deputy head called me down to her office and they were there, all sitting crying. All my so-called friends.

I hate you. I hate you all.

'You're friends are very worried about you, Lynsey.'

Fuck off. Stupid old bag.

I smiled, feigned surprise, but my stomach was curling up inside.
    'They're worried you've not been eating properly,' she continued, 'and members of staff have also said that they've noticed changes...'
    'I'm fine. Absolutely fine.'
    'So there's nothing to worry about then. Nothing you want to tell me.'
    'No, can I go back to my class?'
    'Yes, of course.'

She's going to phone the mother. Fucking bitch. Fucking hate her. Hate all of them.

The mother said nothing when I went home. I knew she knew, though.

WSSSA WSSSA WSSSA

WSSSA WSSSA WSSSA WSSSA

It was all whispers and funny looks when I got home and nobody tried to shove a home-cooked meal down my throat, for a change.

Soon everyone in school will know. They will all know how disgusting I am.

WSSSA WSSSA WSSSA WSSSA

I went back to school the next day. I couldn't face going into the common room or to my classes; I simply sat in the library all day.

'Lynsey, –'

I buried my head in my notepad. Tapped my bottom lip with my pencil. I was trying to write a poem.

Fuck off, I don't want to speak to you.

> I nearly drowned
> In my own thirst.
> The current was so strong,
> It almost burst
> My ~~bubble~~ banks. My bubble
> Was floating through the rapids, alone,

'Lynsey, don't ignore us.'

> Straight into dire straits
> And with deep regrets
> I wished, I'd learned to swim – too late:
> I knew, trouble
> Was about to wash over me.
> So, I gulped – then prayed to Neptune

'We're worried about you.'

> …Then to god,
> For help – how shallow!
> I knew, I'd have to swallow
> My pride. For I'd never bathed in church before,
> I'd always tried to pull the plug on little ~~fish~~ ponds.
> I wanted to make a big splash

'Won't you at least talk to us?'
    'Fuck. Off.'

> Into the sea – instead, I thrashed
> And struggled against the tide:
> The waves were wide
> And wild; And I wished I'd worn my water wings,
> I wished some land lubber
> Would throw me a rubber ring.

'Come on, just –'
    'I said,' I growled, raising my voice slightly, 'fuck off.'

> …Glug…glug…glug…glug…
> I felt as though someone was trying to pull the plug
> ~~On me! The seaweed dragged me under~~
> On me. The seaweed wrapped around my legs,
> My body was drained,
> And the dregs
> Of my mind drifted on;

'For god sake, we're your friends.'
    My head snapped upwards and I stared right into every one of
their sad, concerned eyes.

> Beyond and below the earth,
> Sinking, and I felt my feet almost touch the bottom,
> With my toe nails
> Scraping the sea bed.
> I felt emaciated
> Beside the whales,

'Please, we want to help you.' An arm landed on my shoulder.

> And the sharks,
> Scared they might bring out the knives and forks:

'I said, 'FUCK OFF!'

I slammed both hands down on the desk and pushed myself to stand so abruptly that -

KERRASH

The chair I had been sitting on, flew out from beneath me. Hands shaking, I picked up the chair and waved it, frantically, above my head. There was a loud intake of breath and then little giggles from the first year class who were learning library research skills.

PSST

WSSSA WSSSA WSSSA WSSSA

'Ok, settle down,' said the librarian. He gave me a look as if to say 'take your argument outside' and I replied with a look that said, 'tell them not me.'

'Come on, there's no point in trying to speak to her.'

They tried to speak to me that afternoon but I locked myself in the common room kitchen. I left school early that day and I didn't go back ever again.

I've forgiven them, now. When I think about what I would have done in their situation, I hope I'd have the strength to tell someone.

❧

The gym. A gym. Any gym.

I need to exercise before my legs turn into jelly fat.

I'd been told to keep exercise to a minimum. I had to reach my target weight before the mother and the dietician would let me anywhere near a gym. The gym fantasy was my misplaced motivation for piling on another two stone in weight.

Once I get to the gym, I can do what I like! I'll lose the fat twice as fast.

I deliberated that it was worth being a 'fat bastard' for a few weeks, if it meant that I would lose more weight in the long run. I was enjoying inspecting the local fitness centres in my area and even convinced the Gestapo to let me buy a trial pass for a week (as long as my sister played chaperone).

'I'm not happy about this, Lynsey.'

I don't think your face has ever seen happiness in its life.

'It's only for a week to see if I like it.'

'I'd rather you waited till your weight was more stable.'

'I've put on two pounds since the last time.'

'Yes, but that was a month ago.'

'I've nearly reached my target. Anyway, I'm not going to the gym to lose weight.'

'I should hope not.'

At least, not until I've secured a membership.

'Just don't overdo it.'

A month later the parents reluctantly subsidized my year's membership for the gym, in cash, upfront. 'You'll probably forget to leave money in the bank every month,' laughed the mother.

'Haha.'

Everyone was amazed that I had gained weight so quickly and was being remarkably co-operative for a change. Little did they know, this transitory phase of 'normal behaviour' was merely the incubation period for a kamikaze plan that would see my metamorphic eating disorder change its shape again.

My chosen gym was brightly lit, with glossy black and white photographs of body builders mounted on the brilliant white walls, a strip of charcoal grey carpet that bordered the shiny off-white tiles of the exercise space and led me like a yellow brick road towards the ocean blue door of the ladies changing rooms.

I never liked the changing rooms much. Well, not so much the changing rooms. It was more the getting changed part that I didn't like.

ॐ

I have a dietetic appointment but I can't focus on anything this morning. My mind is as numb as the ice in my boots. The depression I've felt in the past month has subsided slightly but I feel neither happy nor sad. What I'd really like to do is walk in the snow without leaving any footprints.

If I could have any superhero power in the world, I'd like to be able to make myself invisible.

It's Christmas but it doesn't feel like Christmas (at least it will be Christmas in less than six weeks). The bus gets stuck in snow so I phone the hospital on my mobile phone to tell them I'll be late. 'Ok, I'll let her know,' says the receptionist, her voice tinkling with Christmas cheer, 'Be careful now.' The staff are all very friendly and upbeat, I like them.

I'm so glad, I don't have to go back to that other place.

The dietitian reminds me of a quirky little elf. Her fresh, contemporary outlook is very hard-hitting and concise. Playing devil's advocate, she cross-examines my motives for compulsive gym going and diet-coke drinking. Today, we take a different approach to my recovery process as she sums up my progress in the last two years: 'Ok, Lynsey. I think we've come as far as we can. Your weight has been stable for three months and you say you are following the eating plan. I don't think there is any need for you to come back again.' Smiling, she adds, 'Of course, I'll leave the contact open, just in case.'

Yes! Victory!

HURRAH!

❧

Delighted to have wrapped my first ever Christmas present myself (even if it is all rumply and crumply), I smile congratulations then waddle upstairs to find the sticky-uppy-pin-things. I want to surprise the family by pinning up all the Christmas cards.

Still in my pyjamas at twelve o'clock, the phone wails and I have to plummet downstairs to retrieve the call. The mother is phoning to tell me that the roads are cleared.

Good, I can go to the gym.

The novelty of my short-lived Christmas spirit has worn off as I soon forget about Christmas cards and meander back upstairs to find my trainers.

Burning Pain

When the energy rushes through
My body, consuming me,

My mind is on my feet
My feet are on my mind.

I can only find ecstasy
When I indulge in exercise.

I am blinded by endorphins
Stronger than a hit of morphine.

"No pain, no gain"
I chastise my aches,

Detach myself,
Refuse to break.

I will not be defeated!
I feel like a gladiator!

"I am invincible!"
But, I want to be invisible

When the euphoria is over,
Just disappear into the floor.

Compulsive exercise became my replacement for purging and for food restriction. It interfered with my daily functioning: I lied to my friends and cancelled appointments so that I didn't miss a workout; forced myself to go to the gym when I was tired or unwell. I'd go to the gym if I had the flu, risk pneumonia by jogging in the rain. My eating disorders might have been under the thumb but, if I did eat more, I worked myself twice as hard and god forbid if I missed a workout…

If I rest, if I sleep, I will put on weight.

I used excessive exercise as a punishment for eating and gaining weight. I couldn't allow myself to eat unless I exercised. I'd find the time to exercise at any cost: leave college early and forfeit all my other hobbies. I had a gruelling fixation to push myself at all costs.

I was tired all the time but I pushed myself to exercise until I shook with pain and exhaustion because I wanted people to praise me for my self-control in denying my appetite. I equated weight loss with power and achievement. In my mind, the smallest omission from my militant exercise regime would lead to weight gain and the gain of even a pound or two was equivalent to failure:

Dear Ed,

I can't sit still because I can't stop thinking about burning calories. The gym is going to be closed for the Christmas holidays and I'm terrified of gaining weight. I don't want to watch TV or read a book because I'm convinced that if I don't exercise now my muscle tone will melt away into saggy flab and I'll become a couch potato overnight.

I haven't thrown up now in months. I am so happy. I hate Ed. He-She-It is hovering around in the background and I know it, but everything is going to get better because I am going to start a new rehabilitation programme at the brain injury unit.

Easier said than done. I was always making promises to myself.

Exercise dictated the shape of my days. I was often so focused on physical challenge that I forgot exercise was supposed to be fun. I'd measure myself on physical performance and achievement but, deep down, I knew that it was really all about control and self respect. I'd remember how it felt to be poor at sports, having everyone laughing at me.

I hate basketball. I can never judge the ball's position or its speed and

SMACK

The class psycho hits me accidentally-deliberately in the face with the ball.

'DUUUH! You're supposed to catch it,' he screeches, 'not eat it.'

No one ever picks me for their team. I am always the reject substitute. Even at hockey, which I like, or the girls' football team that no one's ever asked me to try out for. No one wants me to play because I hit everyone in the ankles with the ball.

The communal changing rooms embarrassed me, partly because I didn't like my body but mostly because I waged a battle with my clothes. I hated taking a shower because then I had to dry my hair and I ended up looking like I'd had an electric shock.

At school I shied away from post-exercise showers and was always last one out of the changing rooms. I remember rooting around in my school bag ten minutes after the bell had gone, before slowly struggling with my PE kit and tucking my tagliatelle-style laces into the sides of my trainers.

⁓

The sister says I have no dress sense.

Just cause you think everyone should walk around like Britney Spears.

Of course, Nikki is the epitome of fashion herself. It's difficult having a sister who's beautiful when I am so body dysmorphic. I try to like the clothes she likes but she could come home wearing a tablecloth and I'd think she looked great.

'Stop copying me!'

'Leave her alone,' says the mother, 'you can't stop her buying the same jumper.'

To add even more to the sister's disgust, I never seem to carry 'her style' off and I often emerge from my wardrobe like some kind of a cross between a cheap garish pick 'n' mix and a harlequin clown.

'And those are my socks!' she screeches, 'Mum, she's wearing my socks again.'

Well, how was I supposed to know that, if they were in my sock drawer?

I travel to college on a dry, icy winter morning wearing a purple paper-thin Goretex jacket (no gloves or scarf and a perfectly good fleece left hanging in the wardrobe) together with my stone-coloured combats and black dressy shoes with white Winnie the Pooh socks (everyone else at home was in bed or I would never have been allowed out of the door).

Sitting on the bus, mid-journey, I start to realize that perhaps my outfit doesn't quite look right.

Maybe, I should have worn my purple Eeyore socks instead?

Later, on the way home, I get off the bus a stop too early and have to walk the rest of the way. I am so lost in my own thoughts that I almost get mowed down by a dial-a-bus. It is lashing with rain and the bus comes swirling round the corner like a spinning top.

Stupid bus, it's made me get splash marks up the backs of my legs.

The toes of my shoes are scuffed grey; the laces are pulled tight drawing them into my ankles like a noose.

'Look at them,' the mother points, 'you've got them pulled stupid!'

I long for new trainers with laces but I can't tie them right and they make me trip. The mother says I'm better with velcro and buckles.

Just like a baby.

'Stand at peace,' she chastises. She tugs my scarf and tucks it into my furry collar. 'Look, you've got your clothes all up and down like Gourock!'

'Oh what's your hair doing with itself?!' The sister thinks that everyone should walk around with Pantène hair.

It's not my fault it won't brush.

'You'd be quite good looking,' she adds, 'if your hair wasn't such a disaster.'

She doesn't understand. Nobody understands. I've brushed it with my left hand and then with my right and I've tried all the different buttons on the hair frier; I've tried reading hair magazines, I've tried all different brushes and shampoos and conditioners that every hair dresser has ever given me, and still I look like Frizzy Lizzy.

There was a constant fight between the mirror image and the image that I strived to attain. I didn't stop long to celebrate my victories; I simply pushed on to the next challenge.

❧

I still have down days, when I can feel the noose of anorexia tightening around my neck. I wish my thoughts were as clear and easy to see through as the full-length mirror adjacent to my bed. I used to pose for hours, counting my ribs like fine trophies, praising my weight losses – and criticizing my gains. I used to exercise maniacally to maintain a Ryvita-thin dress size six, but people say that the extra few inches of thigh make all the difference to my legs, which once resembled pretzels:

I don't know if it is because I ate chocolate or because my trousers feel a little too tight this morning (my mother tried to fob me off with that fairy story about having shrunk them) or because I honestly believe I am putting on weight. But I do feel fat today. Things don't seem to be getting any easier. I still feel worthless.

What will o her people think of me if I put on weight? There is no time left for friends or family, there is no time left for anything except exercise. I can't stop thinking about the way I look and I can't stop thinking about food.

The dietitian said it would get better – lies, all lies! She promised me. She lied. I can't take this anymore. I can't take any more criticism.

'Don't eat that – You're too fat!

Look at the size of those thighs!

You're pathetic. You've got to be perfect.'

SHUT UP! I scream inside my head. I want to just drop everything. I want to go to sleep and never wake up.

Dear Ed,

So you're back. And you think I'm going to just welcome you back into my life (that's a rhetorical question, I don't want to hear your excuses). You lied to me, you promised me a better life but instead I nearly lost my family. It wasn't just my body you took. You took my friends and everything that was dear to me. I thought it was my fault. I've realized now that you are even more insecure than me. All along, you only wanted to feel superior and point out all my imperfections. I don't need you. I'm building a new life now and you don't feature in my future.

The mother has arrived home from a shopping excursion with Nikki. She bought me a present: a pair of size eight trousers. They fit! I am so happy. In truth, they're actually a tad large but they have a drawstring waist so I can pull them in tight.

Now it's almost lunchtime and the smell of peanut butter washes over me like a general anaesthetic. My greedy eyes water, I start to salivate, I long to spread the peanut butter liberally on a slice of soft, unsuspecting bread. But a gnawing fear inside my head chastises me.

The smell of hot newly made toast is inviting. The kitchen is immaculate and for once the sister is not whizzing around tidying up and droning on about the mess like an erratic Hoover. I have just arrived back from the gym and I can see the mother and the sister through the pane in the living room door, they are eating toasted sandwiches. My own stomach is grumbling but my eye catches a newspaper headline that I must read before I eat. Singer Lena Zavaroni is dead.

It was only a few days ago that I searched on the library computer for a biography of her life. Every time I read a headline like this I have a horrible hollow feeling. My insides flip over, twisting and writhing like a belly full of worms.

When I was just a little girl, my mum says, I used to dance around the living room, singing and clapping to all her old LPs. I grew up loving music: the New Romantic era; Bananarama, Kylie and Jason, New Kids on the Block, Take That.

After my brain injury, the record collection that I'd accumulated over the years did not belong to me anymore. I couldn't remember the singers; I couldn't remember the songs. Then one day, about a year later, I heard a theme song on a TV programme and I couldn't stop singing it. 'I've got that song, somewhere,' said the mother, as she dusted down the sleeve covers of her old records. 'It's called "Swinging On A Star".'

For the next few weeks I played the song so often that I almost wore new grooves into the record. It was another five or six years before I discovered its tragic Scottish singer, Lena Zavaroni. About two years ago, I was sitting reading a newspaper when I came across an article about a former child star who had been accused of stealing a packet of jelly. A few weeks later the same woman, who happened to be an anorexia sufferer, made a public appeal to other sufferers to write to her if they could relate to how she felt. The newspaper article said that she believed eating disorder stemmed largely from depression and a feeling of stolen identity that she called 'static dementia'.

Static dementia. Wow. She wants to have a brain operation to try and take her anorexia away.

I stayed up all night thinking about what I would say to her. Finally, I'd found someone who was experiencing something similar to what I was going through. I never wrote that letter, though. I decided that she'd probably get hundreds of replies and my fear of rejection was as strong as the connection I felt towards her.

My face is burning from the guilt I feel because of the newspaper article I've just read. The mother points out that I looked flushed but I just avoid eye contact with her and meander into the kitchen.

I don't feel like eating any more but I decide to have a small snack. I grab the open carton of oat milk, the dinky little silver milk pan, the jar of Green & Black's organic cocoa and my favourite blue and cream china Tigger mug. I know the cocoa has reached perfection when it froths right up almost spilling over onto the ring.

Skilful me, I have hardly spilled a drop…oops, shit, burnt the pot, again.

I am always burning things and once I even burned the kitchen worktops, two days after the mother had a new fitted kitchen installed. Not long after that I left the pressure cooker on and the sister fought her way through the smoke and turned the gas off.

The day that all my work vanished from my computer, I went out to the gym, leaving the gas on for four hours and the front door unlocked. Later that night, in all the angst and confusion about my missing book, I left a can of juice in the freezer (again) and the next morning woke to find it had exploded.

Dear Ed,
I think, I'm finally learning to let go of you. I had a long lie-in this morning and then I had a normal Sunday brunch with my family. No one mentioned you, in fact you didn't even enter my mind until now. When I went to the gym in the afternoon, I took my time because there was no one there to nag at me or tell me I was lazy. I spoke to people that I hadn't seen for ages and I didn't feel like I was betraying you.

At the end stage of anorexia, there is often brain damage as the body eats into the brain. I guess, I will never know how much permanent damage I have caused and if my memory problems were worsened because of this.

Everyone says my memory is so much better than it was. Is it?

I'm going to be more tidy, more organized, eat healthier, pursue a realistic exercise regime... Blah, blah, blah...

My moods fluctuate. I still punish or reward myself with food. I still push myself to try harder, I'm still obsessed with my weight. Everything revolves around my failures and achievements (and I don't feel like I've achieved much these last few months).

❧

The staff at the gym soon got to know me, and most of the members knew me by name, on account of the amount of time I spent there and the various classes I had joined. I was never quite sure, however, who I was talking to, telling what to, where I'd met them, had I talked to them before, did I know them primarily from the gym?

Where? Why? When? Which? What? Who?

OH WHATEVER!

I learned to agree with people, avoided saying their name or even trying to guess their name out loud.

I always think it's incredibly rude to ask someone their name if you've met them before and I'd hate to think of myself as rude.

I had a sneaking suspicion that the woman that I'd been talking to in the changing room – I'd been telling her about yesterday's adventure in Partick when I'd got lost coming out of a shop – was the same woman who'd given me a lift down to the bus stop the past two Saturdays after the body conditioning class.

But then again, this isn't Saturday... Hmm, don't want to ask in case she thinks I'm nuts...

'Lynsey,' she said, puncturing my wheel of thought.
   'Uh-huh?'
   'Was it an old head injury that caused your memory problems?'

I don't remember saying I had memory problems. Is this a trick? How... What... Does she know me? Has she always known me? Does she know that I don't know she knows me? Or have I told her something I don't know I've told?

'How did you know that?'
   'Oh, my daughter has similar problems. She had a head injury.'
   'Oh.'

Small world.

'Yeah, she was only two at the time.'
   'How old is she now?'
   'She's eight.'
   I stared at her for a moment before tracing back the lines of time. I remembered a day in a shopping centre...

There *was* a woman…a woman in a…
Can't see her face…
She's got pram…a child…a little girl…
I can't see her face…
I can't see the girl's face…
Could it be?
'All that baby does is cry. She had a head injury too,' my mum had said.
'What happened?'
'A bit of a building fell on her head.'

Blinking back the tears, I gasped, 'It was your baby…it was your baby…got the…got the building on its head, wasn't it?'

'Yes, a piece of masonry fell on her head. How did you know that?'

'My mum told me. You know her. You used to give her a lift home from the support group.'

GASP.

Neither of us could believe it. How synchronistic it was that our paths had interwoven. I met her little girl soon afterwards. She was beautiful and looked as bright as any other 'normal' eight-year-old. There were no bruises or fractures, no bandages around her head and no magic wand to reveal her imperfections.

Chapter 8

My Gran

My gran is going daft. 'Jeanie, Margaret, Nicola…umm…Tommy?'
She can't even get my name right. She calls me every other name
under the sun and not one of them is even close. She even calls me by
my dad's name.

And she keeps trying to make me eat meat. I've not eaten meat for
ages and ages. She knows that. 'I've made lentil soup,' she says. I peer
into the suspect pot; there's big pink pig guts sewn onto xylophone
bones.

Icky yucky spewy, I'm not eating that.

The hamstring raft is drowning in the carroty orange rapids; they're
spitting and belching chunks of lentilly gunk.

**Looks like sick. How come there's always carrots in sick, even
when you've not eaten carrots for weeks?**

'It's got ham ribs in it. I'm not eating that!'
'It's ok. I'll take the ham ribs out.'
Well, I didn't eat it; I don't even know how my dad could've
eaten that stinky fish and chips she made the other day. Swimming in
pure grease. Oven chips and frozen fish and she put them in the chip
pan. Even I can always make oven chips. All you do is put the grill on.

No wonder she got food poisoning.

It was a neighbour that found her. They had to call in the emergency doctor. Gran's lost lots of weight; the skin of her cheeks hangs down like that droopy dog, the one from cartoon network that has the real-ly slo-ow a-and de-press-ing voice. She had to get all new clothes as well. My gran used to be a size twenty-two and now a size sixteen is getting too big.

When my mum went through all her food cupboards, she found old tins of cold meat that were four years out of date. She'd been storing them all up like a hamster. 'We'll just have to keep an eye on her, make sure she's eating properly.'

She stopped going out of the house after that. One of the neighbours got her newspaper and her milk and odds and ends at the corner shop; on a Saturday, we would pick up some groceries for her when we went to visit.

I don't like going there anymore. Today, when I went to see her, she wouldn't let me back out of the house.

'Jeanie, Mary, Margaret, Nicola…'

Sigh.

'You've only just got here.'

No, I've been here for nearly three hours.

And she just talks to me about people that were dead before I was born.

'She talks about people that were dead before I was born as well,' says my mum.

'She's getting old,' says my dad, 'she just forgets sometimes.'

The doctor says it's 'moderate dementia' but it's going to get worse.

I couldn't believe it when they said she'd had two strokes. Shock is too mild a word to describe my feelings. Even though I was around stroke victims at the brain injury rehabilitation centre, I had never even considered that my gran might have the same difficulties as them. The concept of my gran having a brain injury was completely absent from my mind. I was too concerned with getting on with my own recovery.

She talks funny, now. Sometimes, I don't even know what she's saying so I just agree. Most of the time, she just sits and swears to herself: 'Hells bells hells bells...' Mumble... grumble... utter... mutter... lament... lament... lament... 'Fucking daft old ... daft old ... fuck-fucking bastard.'

She didn't want a home-help, at first. My gran has always been a very private person and she didn't want strange people in her house. She was scared that people would think her house was dirty. Right up until the day they came and took her away, my gran's house was pristine clean. No dirty dishes, the carpet dust all sucked up in the hoover, no crumbs and all the rubbish down the big metal chute. Everything had a place and everything was always in its proper place. Even the fridge magnets were lined up in a specific regimental order:

1. Three little pigs

    - a jogging pig with a head band

    - a pig standing on the scales

    - a pig weightlifting plates of jelly.

2. The evil clowns

    - green violin clown

    - purple saxophone clown

    - spotty hat clown

    - stripy pyjama clown.

3. Miscellaneous magnets.

The jogging pig always burls round and round and upside down, every time someone opens the fridge door. I slide him over so that he is chasing a marching brown bear with a trumpet. 'No pain, no gain' is what it says on his big piggy pink belly. I slide the pig on the scales on top of one arm of the weightlifting pig and tip him over like he's too heavy on the one side.

This is great fun.

Swiwwiissshhhh

Gran's hand comes flying from behind and wipes out my magnetic picture.

OH.

Swish-a-swish-a-swishy-swish-swish

'He goes there and he goes there and he's been there f-f-for years,' she shrieks, rearranging my masterpiece.

I want to go home now.

She keeps shouting at me and saying the man in the wardrobe is stealing her shoes. She's got more than thirty pairs of shoes with gloves and hats and scarves to match and some of them have never even been out of their boxes. She hides them in cupboards and then forgets where she's put them and then she says they've all been stolen.

She hadn't been out of the house for a year when my mum and I took her down to the Robertson's jam exhibition at Paisley Museum. Her eyes lit up like glow-in-the-dark marbles when she saw the old jam jar labels with the golliwogs. 'M-me...me...g-g-golly-golly ...jam work...'

'She used to make the jam,' says my mum, 'in the old Robertson's jam factory.'

I thought she was getting better. I hadn't seen my gran so happy for years. Well, not since the strokes. I was wrong. The next time I went to visit, she was shouting and swearing and trying to attack her reflection. 'I'm watching you,' she screeched into the mirrored wardrobe. 'You dirty bastard.'

We lived so far away but gran expected us to be there every time she wanted a cup of tea. Even when we sold our lovely big house to be closer to her, it wasn't enough. She needed more care. While three home-helps went in to see her every day, phone calls from interfering neighbours were becoming an everyday occurrence.

'Margaret, is that you?' It was Nosey-neighbour number one.

'No, it's Lynsey.'

'Where's your mother?'

'She's at work.' My mum only worked two afternoons a week while I was out at rehab.

'Well, you'll need to come in.'

'I'm just on my way out.'

'Well, it's an emergency.'

'Why, what's happened?'

She's roaring and moaning down the phone and I don't even know what's she saying. I begin to panic, imagining all hell has been let loose.

'Your gran's kettle's broken and she wants a cup of tea.'

'Well, could you maybe make her a cup of tea and…'

Sigh. Ho-hum.

'I'll tell my mum as soon as she gets home. Thanks for –' CLICK.

Stupid cow. In the time she'd spent on this phone she could have made ten cups of tea.

And then on my mum and dad's twenty-fifth wedding anniversary, the only night that my mum and dad had been out for the past year, Nosey-neighbour number two phones six times:

- 'Hello, Margaret? It's your mother, she says there's someone in her house. Could you phone me back when you get in.'

- 'Hello, Margaret? Your mother wants me to phone the police. Can you phone me back when you get in.'

- 'Hello, Margaret? Are you not back yet? Phone me back when you get in.'

- 'Margaret, it's me again. Can you phone me back.'

- 'Margaret, your mother's asking for you. Give me a phone.'

- 'Margaret, where have you been? I've been phoning all night. You'll need to come up and see your mother.'

I think she must have dementia as well.

Discreetly, mum turned the key like a stealthy cat burglar picking a lock. We stole into the empty house, quietly fastening the door behind us. The floorboards creaked beneath my feet and the hollowness of the walls made me sound like a heavy breather. Apart from the half-full cup of gone-cold tea and the little bit of fluff that had landed on the carpet, everything was just as it should be: covers neatly laid over the backs of the plush velvet arm chairs, dishes secreted away in the cupboards, knives and forks asleep in their drawers and those bloody evil clown magnets set out the way she liked them.

'Lynsey, put those biscuits – the ones that haven't been opened – in that carrier bag.'

I didn't want to do it. They weren't our biscuits.

'There's no point in putting them in the bin. She only ever bought them for visitors anyway.'

I felt like a cheap thief, emptying the last few dregs of the gone-sour milk down the sparkling silver sink.

'Lynsey,' my mum said, blinking back the tears, as we were about to leave, 'do you think we're doing the right thing, sending her there?'

'Mum, you know what the doctor said: "it's the best place for her".'

Clutching my chest, I breathed a huge sigh of relief. My eyes circled her bedroom, one last time, penetrating the dust of the untouched furniture before stopping to rest on the vast vulgar crack in the mirror. As the mist on the grey windows clouded over, all my secreted memories of the hospital came seeping back into my mind like a poisonous gas.

Chapter 9

The Brain Injured Community

When I chucked school for the last time, the mother and I enlisted in a drop-in café for the brain injured community. It was mostly full of stroke victims and men over fifty who all seemed perfectly happy just to sit and drink tea and smoke themselves stupid.

This place is full of old falling apart people.

It reminded me of the village, back at the hospital, where we bought our cigarettes and juice. The Princess, the Vampire and me, we used to walk down to the village everyday because we were allowed out 'on parole' for half an hour.

I don't know why it's called the village 'cause it's not even a real village. There aren't even any houses.

There was a craft shop, a hairdresser's where you could also get your ears pierced – 'Lynsey, I said no already,' growled the mother, 'I don't care if everyone else is getting their ears pierced,' – a newsagent's and a little coffee shop with white plastic tables. It was always overpopulated with patients from the geriatric ward who – it seemed – had nothing better to do but sit drinking tea all day and burning holes in the tables with their cigarettes.

That will be the Vampire in a few years.

'Woooh, look at her with the pink hair,' laughed the Princess.

'Hey granny,' shouted the Vampire, 'where did you get your wig, that's gorgeous?'

'A-away, ya fuck-fucking-fucking…boot yer arses for youse…' Granny-pink-hair shook her cup of tea at us, spilling it over her scrawny bent legs. 'Ahhh, ya bastardin fucking…' She jumped up and shook her fist at us.

'On yourself granny,' shouted the Vampire. The two of them shook with laughter.

'Fuck here she comes,' said the Princess, 'the old psycho.'

She flew towards us, spitting and swearing with her pink hair flap flapping round her ears like chicken wings. 'YAAAAHH!' She screamed right in my face and my heart jumped, I thought I might explode.

'Where you going, you fanny?' The Princess ran after me.

'I don't like it here.'

I never went back to the village. Not even when the Princess offered to pay for my ears to get pierced for the second time.

She's only offering cause the mother says I've not to get them done.

From then on, I got my cigarettes and juice from the garage.

☙

One day, at the drop-in café, I was drafted into playing cards with a man who'd had some kind of organic head injury. He had rolling eyes and a constant stream of saliva dribbling down his chin, and he reeked of stale cigar smoke. 'Yorr a lurrrvly, lurrrvly, a lurrrvly gurrrl,' he kept reciting to me, irritating my ear with the whirring 'r'. 'Worrra yorrra nem?'

I tried to pretend that I hadn't heard him. I hid behind my fan of playing cards to avoid his joogly eyes.

I wish he would shut up.

'Yorrra lurrrvly, lurrrvly gurrrl. Worrra yorrra nem?'
  'He's asking what your name is,' said a tea and coffee volunteer.
  'Oh,' I replied, 'Lynsey.'

CAWCAWCAWKIKICAWHAWHAWHHAAAWW

I watched in horror as his eyes bobbled and his face turned purple, twisting and contorting like a Spitting Image puppet.

Oh my god, he's having a stroke!

Then I realized he was laughing. 'Lynssseee,' he hissed, 'Lynssseee De Paul.'

No, that's not my name.

I left him heehawing and hootsying and shouting, 'Lynssseee De Paul, a lurrrly gurrrl', as I made my escape to the domino table where my mother was sitting slurping tea with the Occupational-hazard, I mean, therapist and looking thoroughly bored.
  'Do. You. Want. To. Play. Dom-in-oes. Lyn-sey.'

I. Am. Nei-ther. Stu-pid. Nor. Do. I. Have. A. Hea-ring. Im-pair-ment.

'Nooo. Than-kuh-yooo.'
  Another day, the mother had taken me to the super market in Anniesland when I clocked the Occupational-hazard flitting between the ice cream and the frozen veg cabinets. I whirled the

trolley out of the mother's hands and tried to do a u-turn back up towards the bakery aisle.

'Lynsey, what are you doing?'

'It's that woman.'

'What woman?'

Too late, she's spied us.

The Occupational-hazard came flying towards us, tripping over her too-tall high heels and doing one of those embarrassing handker-chief waves that says, 'Coo-ee'.

'And. How. Are. We. To-day. Lyn-sey?'

Fine. Till. We. Met. You.

'Fine.'

Brrrrrrrrrr

I stood shivering, pretending to look interested in her lamentations.

Brrrrrrrrrr

The hum of the freezers was making me twitch.

'...and as I said before Mrs Calderwood, you should just get yourself back to work and we'll take care of Lynsey – She's more than welcome to join our art class on a Monday afternoon.'

'Oh, I don't think...'

'Nonsense, she'll love it.'

So I will. There's no way I'm joining any of your basket weaving classes.

I hopped from one foot to the other, clapping my hands together.

'Mu-um, I thought you said you were in a hurry?'

⁊

We all take off our shoes. That's nice and comfy. I prefer not wearing shoes. I take off my socks as well because this floor is slidey: cool, polished wooden floorboards. This place used to be a primary school; this was the children's gym. There's all big mirrors across the room and nothing else. Just mirrors and floorboards and the Tai Chi guy's brought a CD player.

He starts talking but I don't really understand all the mumbo jumbo tai cheesy words.

He might as well be talking in Chinese.

'The history of Qigong…practices date into the time of Chinese shamans…'

Keegong?

'…the practical healing and stress management…tradition in China today.'

Mmmhmm.

'…a deep breath, rest your mind…'

He looks a bit like one of those monk people with that baldy head and the white robes. Maybe not a monk, a harry carry guy or one of those Buddhist folk that stand on the street corner and ask for money then make you say 'gouranga'.

'We're just going to start off with a few relaxation exercises.'

DAAH DAAH DAAAAAH

He turns on this weird Chinesey music: a mixture of pan pipey sounds; running water and birds chirping.

DA DAH DA DAH DAAAAAH

WSSH WSSH CHEEP CHEEP WSSH

Then he starts to massage round his eyes, rubbing round the sockets not the eyeballs like you do when you're sleepy. 'Just gently…making small circles… This first exercise is called "Opening The Chi."'

Cheese! Sounds like cheese!

'…feet shoulder length apart…'
   DA DAH DAAAH
   '…positioning one leg in front of the other…on your right knee…'

I'm not getting this at all. My arms won't go right.

'Ok, it's much easier if you do this.'

That's what I'm doing.

'Try not to bend your other knee.'

This is supposed to be relaxing, why are my arms sore?

'…energy points…focusing on the energy points…'

   EEE CHEE BEE CHEE A-I-YEEE
   EEE CHEE BEE CHEE A-I-YAAH
   A-I-YAAH
   A-I-YAAH
   A-I-YAAH

'And this last exercise is called "Marching while Bouncing a Ball.'

STAMP STAMP STAMP

What a load of elephants this lot are.

I try to lift my hand and foot at the same time. Try to pretend my knee is the ball I'm bouncing. But by the time I've got my arm and leg going at the same rate, they've swapped legs.

This is impossible.

The music's slowed right down.
UM UMM UMMM UMMMM
He gives us out a sheet with a picture of body map with all the outlined energy points and a list of all the exercises. He says if we practise at home, just one exercise a day, we'll soon know them all.

I've already forgotten how to do them. I don't think I'll come back. No, I'm rubbish at this, what's the point?

'That was good,' he says, as I'm walking out the door.
'Eh?'
'Just keep practising that last exercise,' he lifts his knee up in time with his hand like he's pulling it up with an invisible string, 'it'll help improve your balance.'

Opening Chi, Opening Chest, Rainbow Dance, Marching while Bouncing a Ball... I know all eighteen exercises now and I practise every day.

?

Then I forget them all because the Tai Chi guy stops coming.

That's just typical, they finally set up a decent class here at this brain dead place and then it goes and gets cancelled.

Chapter 10

Sexual Identity

'Are you nervous?'

I was, but I didn't want to admit it. He had one hand on my arm and the other on the locker door, blocking my escape.

'I've wanted to do this, ever since I met you,' he said. I shuddered as he leaned in, slapping his cold, wet fish lips onto my lips.

Slurpa – slurpa – slurpa – slluurrrpp!

I could feel my mouth contort as he vacuumed me in like a leech, his slimy, snaky tongue slithering around in my mouth. Waves of saliva were spilling over the corners of my lips and I could taste the packet of peppermint blue Orbit that he had chewed for this occasion.

One...two...three...

I counted, slowly, inside my head. I wondered if twenty was a respectable number to abandon ship?

'Lynsey,' called one of my friends, 'We need to go for our bus.'

Thank you, I am saved!

'It's fine,' he croaked, 'I'll walk her to the bus stop.'

I wished I'd gone with them. I didn't want Froggy to walk me home. I didn't want him or his slimy hands anywhere near me. But I didn't have any choice. Not if I wanted him to keep my secret. He'd told me that he played football with some of the boys from my old school and they'd told him all the amusing tales about the 'memory woman'. He'd promised that he wouldn't tell anyone but I couldn't be sure.

I don't want to do anything (or not do anything) that might upset him.

I gasped as his cold, creepy fingers wriggled like slugs as they crawled through the armpit of my swimming costume.

'Are you nervous?' He hissed, his tongue tickling my ear.

'No,' I lied.

It went on like that all the way throughout school and even when I eventually got to college I still couldn't handle romantic encounters with boys. Gradually, I learnt to cope with friendships with them but kissing felt like a chore, something I had to do to be the same as everyone else.

❧

At seventeen, my bulimic tendencies reached a peak. I was finding it increasingly difficult to cope with schoolwork, peer pressure and the memory impairment and psychological scars caused by my head trauma and my stay in the adolescent unit.

To add insult to injury, the education authorities withdrew my special needs tutor. One day, the poor woman arrived to be told that she no longer had a job. 'Cutbacks' was the unsatisfactory answer. I'd lost my best friend and now I'd lost the only teacher who could understand me.

What's the point of trying? What's the fucking point?

Shortly after my seventeenth birthday, I experienced my first sexual encounter. I had been friends with Gatsby for about a year. I thought he was the perfect best friend: he was quirky and funny and very laid back about everything. We avoided serious issues and I never talked about my head injury or psychological problems. We got drunk together and talked about clothes and music and boys that I fancied and slagged off all the drama queens in youth theatre.

'Did you see me talking to James tonight?'

'Mmm, yeah.'

'I was trying to look really relaxed, I just never know what to say.'

'Just be yourself, he seems like an all right guy.'

'He's really sweet,' I cooed, 'sorry, I'm going to shut up now.'

'I don't mind. I can see why girls might fancy him. He's got good dress sense – I like his shoes.'

I smile, mischievously, 'Why is it more acceptable for a girl to say another girl is pretty but guys can't comment on guys?'

'They do,' he said, sheepishly, 'just not out loud. I don't hang around with nice-looking guys because I always get stuck with their girlfriends' ugly mates!'

Every week we went to McDonalds after drama. He'd always order an apple pie; I'd always order a chocolate milk shake that I'd never finish.

Uggh, why do I buy these things? They taste like the build up drinks the anorexic girl used to get.

Sometimes there were other people from drama but we were always the last two to leave. We would catch the bus home together if we hadn't missed the last bus. If we missed the last bus then we walked.

What the hell, I'm already late.

My perception of him changed, however, when we became lovers. He wanted to get drunk more often, have sex less often and bitch about everyone else in youth theatre more often.

'I want to go and get scuppered.'

'No money,' I replied.

'I'm going to a works night out on Friday.'

I was longing for him to ask me along. I wanted him to show me off to all his friends.

'Where are you going?'

'Club X. It's just guys that are going.'

'Isn't that a gay club?'

'Yeah. But it's got good music and one of my mates is gay.'

I never pursued the issue any further.

Why on earth would I want to go to a gay men's club?

For some strange reason I thought only men could be gay. I had never met a gay woman. I still felt a little left out but I also felt relief that no other girls would be going to Club X.

Pink Egg Dreams

He's walking on eggshells,
Hiding his true colours
From a cracked world.
Where mannequins blow raspberries at men
Who like roses and lavender scents,
It makes sense for him
To wear slip-on shoes with laces.
All made up in pink fancies,
Another face is born
Through the looking glass.

NEWS FLASH. Gatsby is GAY! My sister told me. Her best friend lives in the same street as him.

I felt like he had taken something from me. Three years after I'd split from Gatsby, the past had come back to haunt me, and this was one skeleton that I wished had stayed in the closet. Never for a moment did it cross my mind that maybe, just maybe, it was all a mistake. That, maybe, it could be a rumour. Oh no, I had it all worked out. I had all the proof: he went to gay clubs, had gay friends, thought other men were nice looking.

I've turned him gay. I must be so horrible and that's why he's turned gay.

I hungered for people to touch me yet I could not bear to be touched. Even years later, when I started college, when people hugged or kissed me I froze. It drove me deep inside myself. It wasn't that I thought Gatsby was disgusting. I thought I was disgusting. I tallied it up as another black mark against my character and decided, subconsciously, that I would become androgynous.

∾

Later, when I was in rehab, I began a romance with another client at rehab. He was six foot tall, part Canadian, with boyish good looks and only an inkling of stubble. He used to wait for me after I finished work and we'd go for a coffee at Cathy's café.

I haven't had a decent coffee from the café on the corner since Cathy from college who worked in the café got promoted to manager in another branch. I used to like Cathy's café. It was right on the corner of the street next to my bus stop. Cathy always used to make the tip-toppiest lattes: just one shot of coffee, soya milk at the perfect temperature, a nice amount of froth on top and she never spilled any on the saucer. Cathy knew how I liked it; I didn't even have to ask. (I hadn't drunk coffee for years until I met Cathy. Not since I stopped drinking milk.)

Black coffee tastes like tar.

Then Cathy told me that they sold soya milk.

Soya milk, great stuff!

I can't remember how we first got talking. She wasn't even in any of my classes. I think she was just a friend of a friend of a friend or something. Media in the Communications Industry, I think that was what she was studying. I knew one person on that course (I can't remember her name now) and she introduced me to everyone else over lunch one day.

Cathy was veggie as well. Not vegan, though. She ate eggs but not milk. She said she was, 'instrumental in introducing soya milk into the whole chain of coffee shops'. She said she was planning to turn vegan eventually but her downfall was beer. 'Inside the pub, my principles go out the window. I'd drink paraffin if they put it in a pint tumbler!'

I remember the day she got her hair cut short. Really short and spiky: blonde spikes, six inches high. Just as I was leaving, she came hurtling into the college cafeteria like Sonic the hedgehog gone peroxide. I doubled back, saying, 'I really love your hair. Smart!' I wanted to touch it, try and ruffle it, see if the spikes would bounce back up on their own accord.

I've never seen a girl with hair as spiky as that.

'Do I look like I've got a spiky-dykey-do?'

Eh?

'A what?'
    'Does my hair look dykey?'
    'Very spiky.'

'But does it make me look like a dyke?'

Uhh? Sounds like something they used to say on *Prisoner: Cell Block H.*

'I think it looks wicked.'

'I just got chatted up by an older woman there,' she said, edging her way into a different conversation.

'Where?' I said, wanting to nurse the scandal.

Cathy was pretty. Feminine. She wore lipstick and eyeliner and I'd even seen her wear a dress on occasion. She certainly didn't fit in with the stereotypical butch dykes in dungarees from my favourite 1980s TV programme. She had recently 'come out' to me when, mid-conversation, she nonchalantly mentioned the fact that she and her new girlfriend were going to the college night out and they would meet me so that we could all go together. 'Oh,' I said, 'right.' I laughed to myself.

How slow am I?

Then again, I had supposed when I first met her that she might be gay but I'd been led to believe otherwise when during a conversation we'd had about how I could 'get rid' of the Canadian she'd said, 'Introduce him to me.'

The next day, Cathy's older woman tried to chat me up in the caf. I left swiftly, twirling my pigtails and wondering if perhaps this was where I was going wrong with men?

Maybe, I look like a 'dyke'.

I'd been friends with the Canadian for months before he'd asked me out on a date. He was romantic, charming, not like the immature clown boys I'd gone to school with. Something wasn't right, though.

I let him put his arm around me when we walked down the street but whenever he tried to kiss me, I shrank back.

What is wrong with me?

I tried talking to Cathy about it but I couldn't explain how I felt. I didn't know how I felt. There was something very wrong but I just couldn't put my finger on it. 'Hey, if you don't like kissing guys,' said Cathy, 'why don't you try girls?'

URRGH

I was horrified at the thought that Cathy could think that I might be - that I might be - that I might be - gay? - a dyke like her? 'I'm not gay!' I screamed, 'Do I look gay to you?' 'I don't know,' she replied, sarcastically, 'what does a gay person look like?'

Straight Acting Girl

Just 'cause I don't wear Doc Martins
Or drink a dozen bottles of
Miller, then burp 'n' fart 'n' spit
To punctuate every swear word,
Doesn't mean I can't fancy girls.

Who says I can't wear baby pink,
Wear bunches in my hair? Think it's
Up to me if I decide to
Read *Elle* 'stead of *Diva*. Why
Should I hide my feminine side.

So I don't look like a lesbian,
But how do you look gay? Is there
A dictionary description?
I'd really like to know what a
Dyke's meant to look like, anyway.

She was my friend and I'd never been homophobic before, but suddenly all the old thoughts of Gatsby and how his revelation had rocked me, came spewing back into my mind. 'Hey, I was only kidding,' she said, 'but, just take it slow, tell him you're not ready.' I was nearly twenty-one years old. Was I ever going to be ready?

❧

'Who are you?' said the Caterpillar.
This was not an encouraging opening for a conversation.
Alice replied, rather shyly, 'I—I hardly know, sir, just at present — at least I know who I was when I got up this morning, but I think I must have been changed several times since then.'

Alice's Adventures in Wonderland, Chapter 5

It's not so much 'who', more like 'what' was Alice?
It was goodness-knows-what-time in the afternoon and Alice was goodness-knows-where. Zie'd* started walking into Partick for zie wanted to clear zir** head: Zie'd been having the queerest thoughts over the past two weeks.

It had been an ever-so-bright but arctic afternoon when zie'd set off, but now, an icy wind was tearing through the sky in a most frightful manner; the heavens had just opened up all-of-a-sudden and Alice – well, zie didn't even have a jacket – zie just kept on walking through the never ending anonymous streets of Glasgow's West End because zie just knew that zie had to find the answer to this curious predicament.

Alice had been through the whole eat-me-drink-me situation; swapped bulimia for anorexia, and anorexia for exercise addiction;

---

*   Zie = he / she
**   Zir = him / her

just when it seemed like zie was beginning to get a handle on zir teapot and form normal relationships – although one could hardly call zir twice-weekly sexual encounters with the March Hare 'normal' – it looked like some other fucked up dysfunction was about to rear its ugly Cheshire cat head (and that just wouldn't do at all).

True, there had always been a hint of androgyny in Alice's name and of course, zir character: The early onset of bulimia at 15 had sent Alice's menstrual cycle into disarray and halted the beginnings of zir feminity and any budding sexual appetite. But all the other girls at school had boyfriends so Alice played along. Alice was a girl, after all – At least, that's what zie was led to believe.

Zie tried to ignore the ugly fatty deposits that were burgeoning in zir school-girl shirt, the offensive bleeding that came without warning – sometimes every two weeks, sometimes every three months – and the hideously scary curves that seemed to be dispatching themselves, unflatteringly, all over zir body like the hard shoulders of a motorway. No, zie didn't like any of it, not one bit.

And when zie finally got the hang of the eat-me-drink-me game, zie was just beginning to enjoy being small: zir neatly aligned new hip bones shone through zir skin. so straight zie could wear age eleven boys' jeans. Then they told Alice that zie was not a well girl at all, and if zie didn't start eating properly right this instant then zie would shut up like a telescope!

Alice didn't really care if zie shut up like a telescope, in fact, zie didn't care if zie disappeared altogether: zie thought it would be rather fun to become invisible. However, it soon became very lonely as none of Alice's school friends could see zir anymore and they soon forgot all about zir. This made Alice very sad and so zie decided, zie would try to follow all the curious rules of the hospital, no matter how peculiar they were. And even if zie did come out like a giant, zie would still be the same Alice inside, wouldn't zie?

But who or what was Alice? Zie was hoping to ascertain the answer to this most peculiar question on zir journey down Dumbarton Road and the surrounding streets. During the latest sexual encounter with the March Hare, he'd suddenly professed his love for zir: while he was sinking into seventh heaven, Alice was sinking into the sheets in a state of shock and disbelief. Of course, zie knew that zie didn't love him and no matter how hard zie tried, zie would never see him as anything other than a six foot, real life cuddly toy.

All Alice had ever wanted was a walking, talking, life-size dress-me-up doll that zie could carry around on zir arm like a trophy and then put back on the shelf when zie was finished playing.

The rain was firing down and Alice could feel pinpricks at the backs of zir eyes. As tear drops and raindrops met and linked arms, Alice pressed defiantly against the harsh wind. The gay friend of a gay friend passed by on the same strip of pavement and Alice averted zir eyes. 'Goodness, I hope she didn't see me,' thought Alice, 'I look positively dreadful.'

Looking back, Alice pondered that from a distance, that girl looked positively like a boy. 'Perhaps,' zie thought, 'I am really a boy? For I've always preferred the company of boys.'

It was true that most of Alice's best friends had been boys but, sooner or later, they had all progressed to 'kissing friends'. Alice never meant for any of them to mutate into boyfriends but, frightened they would disappear, zie co-operated with the whole kissing nonsense – After all, all the other girls liked it; eventually, zie managed to tolerate it and sometimes – sometimes, when zie took a swig from the drink-me bottle – zie felt floaty and peculiar and ever-so-happy that it didn't really matter anymore.

'Perhaps,' zie thought, 'one is gay? For if one does not feel attraction towards boys, then one must surely be attracted to girls?' So Alice thought about all the girls zie'd ever known and all the boys zie'd ever known and all the boys zie'd ever kissed and all the girls zie'd ever thought about kissing…

But none of the boys nor any of the girls that Alice had ever known, seemed particularly kissable. 'Curiouser and curiouser,' zie thought, 'one cannot possibly be gay if one does not feel attraction to the same sex. But then, one cannot possibly say one was bi-sexual when one feels no sexual attraction at all!'

The rain and Alice's molten tears had dried right up and Alice was standing in a clear grey puddle, in a strange street. 'Oh bother,' zie said, 'I do believe I have lost my way home!' Zir shoes and socks were soaked right through and zir mobile phone battery had run out. 'Oh dear,' zie said, 'that's what happens to curious little girls who follow funny looking white rabbits.'

So Alice turned right around and walked back through all the puddles until zie came to a caf where a peculiar little man was smoking a hookah. And there zie sat, drinking coffee and writing down all zir curious thoughts in even more curious manner: For Alice liked to write backwards - from left to right - 'That way, zie mused, 'they might come out looking normal.'

$$\infty$$

'I was fourteen or fifteen when I first started to feel attracted to girls,' said Cathy. 'When I was fourteen, I didn't even know what foods I liked to eat.' 'Exactly. You can't catch up on your whole life in seven years.' 'What you mean?' 'Well,' she replied, 'no wonder you feel a bit immature: what you're going through, it's like going through puberty without the spots.'

Chapter 11

Rehab + College

As soon as I had turned eighteen, I was eligible to be put on the waiting list for brain injury rehabilitation. However, it was a full year before my name had clambered into top position; by this time I was neck deep in my various eating disorders, having frequent panic attacks and could hardly hold a conversation. Luckily, they kept my place open and I began attending the centre about six months later for stress management and relaxation techniques.

Them at the rehabilitation centre, they all think I'm 'too tense', 'too anxious'. 'We think you'd benefit from our Thursday afternoon relaxation group.'

I don't think I'm going to like this.

Funny that, they said the same thing when I was in that mad hospital, 'We think you'd benefit from our Thursday afternoon relaxation group.'

Starting to get a wee bit déjà vu here.

Funny that, both groups were on Thursday afternoons.

The first time, when I was in the hospital, I went along nonchalantly. I'd never been to a relaxation group. The teacher-woman was wearing white baggy clothes. Actually, come to think of it, it was really just the occupational therapy woman dressed up – she had her hair all loose and splaying all over the place like silly string curling in the wind.

They're always trying to trick you in this place, changing their hair.

And then she turned the lights out on us. Well, I didn't like that.

What if the Vampire sneaks up behind me?

Then she lit all these mad miniature candles. They were short round dwarves made of wax, wearing girdles round their fat little waists.

That's ok. I'll be able to spy her if she creeps in.

'Ok, we're going to begin with some simple breathing exercises. Just lie down on your mats with your arms by your sides and close your eyes – Lynsey, lie on your back.'

I hate lying on my back. I always think someone's going to jump on my stomach and squash me. Specially, if it's the Vampire. I'd end up like *Flat Stanley* 'cause she weighs ten million tons.

'Breathing deeply, in through your nose and out through your mouth…' I don't know what happened next. That occupational therapy woman was shaking me and saying that was it finished. And did I enjoy it?

Enjoy what? We never did anything except lie down.

She'd switched the lights back on and everyone was putting their mats away.

I'm tired.

My legs and arms were like lumps of lead and my feet had cramp and my fingertips were tingling like Christmas tree lights that had gone on the blink.

'You look like you've just smoked a joint,' laughed the Princess.

Smoked a joint? My joints feel all smokey!

So that was me, my first relaxation class sent me to sleep.

Don't hold out much hope for rehab's efforts to try and keep me awake.

Rehab's relaxation group morphed every week. They called it 'alternative therapy' and every week they had an alien practitioner who would come in and give demonstrations:

Week 1: Reflexology

I thought it sounded good. I thought it was to help make your body more flexible but it turned out it was just some woman who came in and touched your feet.

She isn't touching my feet! Heebie jeebies. Don't like people touching my feet.

It was good, though, watching it. She told us that the big toe is linked with the brain.

My mum broke her big toe that time she fell down a drain. I always thought she was a bit funny in the head after that!

Week 2: Aromatherapy

I would've liked it better if I could smell the smelly stuff properly. Ever since the brain injury, my sense of smell has been suppressed. I have to practically dip my nose into a perfume bottle to even get a vague whiff. It has improved since I began taking the herb ginkgo biloba, however, my nose is selective and only chooses to recognize things like smelly curries, smelly fish, baked beans and peanut butter.

Gin – thingmy – bubble is supposed to help your

I kept forgetting

It was ok for the first couple of weeks but when the jar of tablets ran out, I forgot to… I can't remember who it was that recommended it in the first place. I just remember going into the health shop.

'I'm looking for a herb but I can't remember what it's called.'

'Ginkgo biloba?'

'That's it! What's it do?'

'It increases the circulation of the blood to the brain and therefore aids the memory.'

I don't think this stuff's doing anything for my memory but I'm recognizing all sorts of smells.

Week 3: The Alexander Technique

Someone came in to teach us how to sit on a chair. 'Straighten your back,' she says, 'you'll end up with problems later on in life.'

Hmmph, I was all comfy there. I thought this class was all about relaxation?

My hairdresser calls me a 'slouch'. Sometimes, I get tired holding my head up and tip it to one side. Then he says, 'You're a right slouch!'

Week 4: Visit from Community Art Students

Some art students came to to talk us about a special community project they'd compiled as part of their course.

Week 5: A Visit to the Students' College

The day got divided into five parts. First we played team-building games to get to know each other. Splitting into teams took forever and then some, because certain people couldn't count their team number and the numbers went all wrong. Eventually, we had five groups of six with two students in each group. Each group was given a skinny roll of yellow sellotape and a newspaper and we had to build a tower that could stand up by itself. The idea was to work as a team and try and find the solution before the time ran out. Our tower won. It was my idea.

Next came Art Therapy. We made ugly mugs from clay. Between the behavioural unit, the hospital and the phobic unit, I had become an expert in clay and dough and all things squidgy. Mine might not have been the ugliest face but it was certainly the prettiest and the most precise.

The last part of the morning comprised music therapy. A chance to play bongo drums, coconut shells and glockenspiels.

This is great! I'm brilliant at this!

CLOMP–CLOMP, CLIP–CLOP, TING–DING, CLOMP–CLOMP, CLIP–CLOP, CLOMP–CLOMP–CLIP-CLOP, CLOMP –CLOMP, CLIP-CLOP, TING–DING, CLOMP–CLOMP–CLIP–CLOP– TING–DING–CLOMP–CLOMP– DONG–CLOMP–DONK!

Uhh! Stoopid dumstick bounced an hit by dose.

After lunch, we tried drama therapy.

Easy peasy japanesey!

We danced and pranced all round the room to moody saxophone music and made up our own words:

DA-DA-DAH DA-DA-DAH-DAAAH

DA-DA-DAAAH DAAAH DAAAH DAAAAAHHH

It was more simplistic than my first day at youth theatre but I was high as a giraffe on stilts and this was the first day since I'd came to rehab that I hadn't been falling asleep!

In the last hour, our clay heads were baked and ready to come out of the oven. I didn't like the shit yellow and brown or the snotty green paint so I left mine baldy and grey as a gargoyle.

As the rest of them slobbered paint around their gumsy master-pieces, I waltzed round, happily, talking to the students. 'Did you enjoy yourself then?' said a girl with panda eyes. She was wearing a spiky dog collar and her hair was raven black with an electric blue streak down the middle.

'Brilliant! I'd love to do a course like this.'

'You should go to college and do your highers.'

'I've already got two highers.'

'I think you'd get a lot out of this course.'

'Is there any writing therapy on your course?'

'Writing therapy?'

'I want to write poetry for people to act out.'

'Maybe you'd be better doing a performance arts course.'

That's what I want to do, performance poetry, but I'll never remember the words.

That's when I knew. Just like the other Lynsey, I wanted to be an author and an actor; no other job would do. Finally, I could accept we had something in common.

College! I'm going to college! I'm not sure if I'm ready for this but it's only one class. Creative writing. Tuesday morning. Not exactly missing much at rehab.

The creative writing class was ongoing, so I returned the following term. My confidence was growing and I was ready to take on more classes in creative drama and film studies. I was still attending rehab so my week was the fattest it had been since high school.

There was a complete shake up in my rehabilitation program. Relaxation group was swapped with psychology and my creative writing class had been changed from a Tuesday morning to a Friday and this meant missing the ten-pin bowling or other leisure activity at rehab. However, I'd began working on my ultimate ambition and that was to write my autobiography. I was beginning to accept the new challenges that were being thrown at me and I was ready to face the society that had cast me out at last.

My parents bought me a word processor of my own and, later, a PC with a larger memory capacity, on account of my loyalty to my writing.

Tap, tap, tap-tap

Tap, tap, tap-tap-tap

I worked everyday like a trouper. What started off as therapy soon became a mission.

I'm going to show them all I can do it. All the people, all the teachers who said I was rubbish.

'What's your novel about?'
'It's an autobiography.'
'An autobiography at your age? What have you got to write about?'

Tap, tappety-tap

Tap, tappety-tap

This book isn't about me anymore...it's about...it's about... educating people... If I can save one kid from going through what I went through...

'Lynsey, it's three o'clock in the morning.'
 'Uh-huh!'
'Lynsey, will you turn that computer off.'
 'Mmhmm.'

Tap-tap-tap

Tap-tap-tap

I tapped my inner most thoughts into the computer's brain for a year till, finally ...

TAP-TAP-TAP-TAP-TAP. TAP-TAP.

CLICK.

HURRAH! FINISHED! 62 THOUSAND 4 HUNDRED AND 80 WORDS.

Click. File. Scroll down. Save. Click.

Error.

→←△△⇨→⇨ ↔⤢⤿⇨▶▷
⇨↑⇨↑⇨▷⇦ ⇨←↓↕⇨↓←←
↳▽⇦▷⇨←▽⇨▲◤⇨↵↑↓↕

Rescuing doc.3

Restarting Windows 98

Oh great, that's me lost about 800 words. Everything I did today. Hmmph. Where's all my work gone?

'There's nothing you can do. The entire memory's wiped.'

Just like me then, eh.

**STUPIDCOMPUTERSTUPIDCOMPUTERSTUPIDFUCKI
NGSTUPID
HORRIBLESTUPIDWHYWHYWHYNOW
WHYWAITTILLITWASFINISHED
WHYYOUHAVETOGOANDDOTHISTOME
HATEYOUHATEYOUHATEYOU**

I couldn't remember what I'd written. The notes were all wiped out as well. It was as though someone had come along and stolen my memory all over again.

I can't start again, I just can't.

'CAN'T CAN'T CAN'T CAN'T CAN'T CAN'T DO IT.'

It felt worse than the time I'd written a diary on a disk and a friend had stolen it. We'd often swapped computer games and she'd spied my disk marked:

TOP SECRET – GET LOST NOSEY PEOPLE

'What's that?'

'Diary.'

'Can I read it?'

'No.'

'Oh come on.'

'NO!'

Later that night, I couldn't find my diary so I phoned the friend. 'Hi, have you accidentally picked up my diary when I gave you those computer games.'

'Huh, no.'

'Could you maybe look because I can't find it.'

'Are you accusing me of stealing?'

'No, I think maybe I gave you it by mistake.'

'Well, I've not got it.'

Two weeks later: 'This is yours, I found it.'

When I put my diary disk into the computer, there was no documentation. It was completely blank.

All my memories. All my memories gone again.

'Can't. Can't do it. Can't remember what to write.'

'You can't give up now. Think of all the hard work you put in.'

SIGH.

Tap.

Tap, tap, tap.

'Who are you?' said the caterpillar.
This was not an encouraging opening for a conversation.
Alice replied, rather sh

❧

As per usual, my period of optimism was short lived and before long, I gave up writing my book and was back to my old self-doubting ways. College wasn't quite going the way I wanted it.

Nothing ever goes right for me.

It was like being at school, the same problems with learning coursework were arising.

I could never distinguish the information I was supposed to learn from the other words that were spoken. If someone was whispering in a corner
'Did you see that film about…'
while the teacher was explaining something or
'Where did you go at the weekend?
the conversation deviated to a comment made about the weather,
'and guess who's away to Turkey for their holidays'
suddenly that was amalgamated into my understanding of the lesson.

And it wasn't that I thought the lessons were boring, it was just that I found it extremely frustrating when there was a particular subject I wanted to learn about but I couldn't seem to stay focused. I would either fall asleep or simply wander off to another planet in my head.

I could be gone for

ten seconds

or ten minutes

and in that time, I couldn't even remember what

'time of day is it?'

I'd been thinking about.

In less stringent classes such as art, where I felt less restricted, I would drive the teacher crazy by tapping my pencil and shifting round to see what other people were doing. I would shout out or wander round the class, commenting on everyone's work. It seemed he was happier when I disappeared for huge periods of time, looking for 'inspiration'.

This art of distractibility followed me through school and onto my attempt at a college course.

YAP YAP YAP...

Lectures were almost impossible to understand. We'd sit for maybe two hours at a time and I'd want to go to the toilet or get up and walk around because sitting listening was making me feel drowsy. I'd try to explain to the learning support staff and I'd be blessed with half-irritated answers like 'Oh, every one switches off at times,' or 'No one remembers everything that is said.'

Yes, but I hardly understand a word they're saying.

Their first attempt to remedy this came in the form of a 'buddy' who was supposed to take notes and photocopy them for me except, they forgot to introduce us. 'Oh, it was supposed to be discreet,' said the learning support person.

So, discreet I didn't know who he was?

He lasted about a week before he started dropping off from class.

'I'm sorry, I can't make students turn up,' was the reply.

So I tried taking my own notes or getting miscellaneous notes off of whoever would lend me theirs. I ended up with a variety of strange squiggles and multi-slanted handwriting that took days to decipher.

Next was the dictaphone. So clever a contraption that it could pick up a sneeze from a hundred yards. But the lecturer's voice was often muffled and it was the same old scenario where I'd fall asleep before it even reached the end of the tape.

☙

Recently, I came across an old photograph of myself as a five-year-old goldilocks. 'That was your first day at school,' said my mum. I was standing outside the gates of my old primary school, wearing my big pre-eye operation spectacles, my new uniform and looking like a right 'Little Miss Perfect'. There was another little blonde girl with the same burgundy blazer and tie, grey pinafore and white knee-high socks.

'And do you know who that is?'

I couldn't believe it when she revealed the identity of the other little blonde girl. The angel-faced child in the photo is now a mother of three and an ex-drug addict, following a methadone programme. How quaint, I thought, the way our lives have been shaped. It turns out we are both in a kind of rehab.

I learnt a lot at rehab. Mostly from the other clients.

The craft of confabulation

This covers:

- how to use memory loss selectively

- how to erase and rewrite history effectively

- how to cut and paste other people's memories

- how to confuse people who can otherwise store information, efficiently.

My friend Brian is the master confabulator. A chameleon when it comes to hiding his memory blips. He taught me how to camouflage my memory deficits by confabulation, replacing lost details and events with imaginary ones, often formulated on the spur of the moment.

I got so good at filling gaps when accurate details were not immediately available, that I often not only misled others but also convinced myself that colourful half-truths and exaggerations really did happen the way I retold them. It requires language and social skills and definitely takes practice to be an expert confabulator. Brian has the gift of the gab.

Wandering round Glasgow in our lunch hour. We are desperately searching for Cathy's coffee shop. Five minutes from rehab and we were here only yesterday.

It can't have closed down already? Someone has stolen the coffee shop?

'Excuse me,' says Brian, capturing a flustered passerby. 'We arranged to meet some friends in the city centre…' I stand there like a totem pole with my mouth hanging open as an entire fairy tale trips off his tongue.

Oh my god, what's he talking about? I can't believe she's falling for this. She actually thinks we're tourists.

The woman nods sympathetically and ten minutes before the end of lunch we arrive at Cathy's cafe, gulp down some hot coffee and then meander back to rehab.

Of course, it can also go the other way: one day Brian stopped to talk turkey with the *gouranga* woman who accosted us on Sauchiehall Street and we ended up with an invite to a vegetarian feast at a Buddhist retreat.

Oh my god, we're going to end up in a cult, now.

One of my own favourite lines to emerge when I forget the name of a recent acquaintance: 'I'm sorry, I've forgotten your name...' The name-shy person will then proudly tell me their name and I will bat my eyes in earnest and reply, 'No-oh, your second name, silly.' This never fails to make the other person slightly embarrassed and helps to hide my own disconcertion.

PLEASE NOTE: this does not work for people you have met more than half a dozen times or for members of your own family.

There is one girl who used to be in my year at school before I had my brain injury who never passes me by. Everyone used to laugh at her because she wore hand-me-downs and everyone said she was stupid because she was in remedial classes. I used to feel sorry for her, but now I smile every time I think about her because she rose above all the comments from the school idiots and made a decent life for herself. It doesn't matter when or where I meet her or how much of a hurry she's in, she always has time to stop and pass the time of day.

'It won't be long now,' she sighs, patting her swollen stomach. 'Next time you see me, I might be pushing a pram.'

'You'll make a great mum,' I say, wholeheartedly.

'Well, this baby was carefully planned. I'm all settled in my wee house and we're hoping to get married next year.'

'Will you go back to work?'

'When the baby's grown up a bit, I'll go back to work part-time,' she adds, 'I had a good job working in the photographers but I gave it up to have the baby.'

'Quite right,' I smile, 'What does your fiancé do?'

'He's got a good job,' she replies, a little defensively, 'He's a forklift driver. He'll be good to the baby. I see all the ones we went to school with and some of them are taking their kids to school...'

Yeah, and some of them have got three and four kids by five different fathers.

I remember her from school, at least. She had a hamster too. She got it for her sixteenth birthday. Can't remember its name, though. A cute little thing. Then someone dropped it on its head. It died of brain damage, I suppose.

Our fish, it's got brain damage as well. The story isn't a real memory of mine but I've heard it so many times: on Nikki's seventh birthday, she was given a goldfish. So excited about the prospect of having her own pet, she ran up the stairs to show it off; tripped on the front stairs and the poor thing was splattered all along the path. My dad scooped it up, out of all the mud and debris and ran up to the house with it, where he deposited it in the first available basin of water: in with all the dirty dishes.

'Lucky', is now eleven years old and fit as a fiddle: it does Callanetics (underwater aerobics) and has attempted to escape. The companion fish is a meagre three years old - someone named it 'Hamish' at one point. But it's relapsed back to its old name: untitled.

If I were an animal, I'd probably be a goldfish because they have a three-second memory span. I'd swim around and around the little underwater tree in the middle of the tank, singing, 'This is a lovely place, I've never been here before... this is a lovely place, I've never been here before...'

The mum-to-be goes off on a tangent here, asking me if I remembered such and such who sat next to whatzisname that used to be in my class for whatzitcalled – that subject I don't remember taking. She doesn't seem to comprehend that I am oblivious to all these names and I simply nod or shake my head in the right places saying, 'Umm, I think I know who you mean,' or 'I'm sure I'd remember their faces if I saw them.' There's no point in explaining about my memory problems. She didn't understand about my brain injury when we were at school and now she's probably forgotten.

'Two and three kids – and they've no one to support them,' she continues, 'At least I'm in a stable relationship.'

'Yeah, twenty-one's far too young to have all those kids.'

'At least my man will support me. He'll stand by me, so he will. At least he's not a junkie. He likes the occasional drink but doesn't go mad with it. He's not an arsehole!'

'No, not like some,' I agree. 'You did the right thing.'

'Did you hear about...'

SUCH AND SUCH... BLAH... BLAH... BLAH...

And she goes on to tell me more scandal about people from my past life that I'm supposed to know.

Brains are just like computers. That's what the doctor told me years ago. If you drop a computer on it's head, the chances are, it won't work right. It's the same with mobile phones. When I first got my phone, I kept dropping it. Everyone at rehab's got a mobile phone. Well, nearly everyone. You're not allowed to turn them on in the building but everyone forgets and all these mad tunes ding-dong-ding every five minutes.

I wanted a mobile phone as well. 'Then I can phone home if I get lost.'

My mum wasn't convinced. 'Lynsey, you'll probably leave it on a bus.'

SIGH.

Text messages received and sent on the way to rehab:

23 March 10:28

Dozat mean ur makn n appearanz 2d? Y, by the way 2 (Lsr Quest)

Brian

Laser Quest? Laser Quest? Weren't we there yesterday?

I get more bruises from walking into the mirrors in *Laser Quest* than I do from falling out of bed in the morning. And the guns, I always get the rubbish ones that don't shoot.

Ihatethewayhejoinsupallhiswordsandnumbersintextmessages

23 March 10:31

Still waiting on a bus. If bus doesn't come soon I will be late. Fucking great bus service... Not!!!

Lynsey

Hey, the Glasgow bus is going the wrong way! That's my bus!

I'm standing on the wrong side of the road.

Rehab also showed us how to set up an email account and use the Internet.

Date: Fri, 17 April 2000 16:09:55 0100 (BST)+
From: 'BrianBeastCan'
To: 'LynseyC'

Hey Lynsey,

A taxi ran over my mobile, which was a bit of a
bugger. I can still make & receive calls on it but I
think the message thing is broken.

B.

Unable to receive and process information, efficiently. A bit like us then, eh?

Running late. On my way to hospital. Bus taking too long. Stupid mobile phone starts to screech. Sigh.

Only bought the stupid thing for emergencies, didn't want anyone to phone me.

I jiggle around in my seat like a constipated worm, trying to retrieve the phone from my stupid bag.

Oomph. Humph.

I struggle to answer it as my stupid bag is zipped and the stupid sticky velcro carrier-case-thing is too hard to open even when I'm not wearing stupid gloves (lost two pairs of gloves and half a pair of slippers this week).

1 missed call

'Mmmm, stupid thing!'

Redial last number

'Hello, who phoned me there?'

'Is that you, Lynsey.'

It was the occupational therapist from rehab that answered. She'd phoned to ask why I had missed my last two appointments.

'Uh-huh, mmhmm…no…yes…right, fine, bye.'

As usual, I'd got my dates muddled and I wasn't even carrying my stupid diary.

'Stupid. Stupid. Stupid.'

'Lynsey, what are you moaning about now?'

'Stupid thing doesn't even work right.'

Your vocabulary is appalling,'

'Hmmph.'

'And you want to be a writer.'

'Well, it's crap then.'

Then the stupid bus lurched and my mum huckled me out onto the street by my stupid bag straps.

Time has a laxative effect on me. I am always rushing. Never enough time. Not enough hours in the day. Always got one eye on the clock. So aware of the rhythm of my champion racing heart rate, I'm terrified that one day soon I'll have a heart attack. Forever on the edge of worry and paranoia, I live by a continuous compact timescale. I'm so busy setting goals and limits, I don't have time to relax and I rarely finish the tasks I impose.

'Relax. You need to relax'. Everyone keeps telling me that but I *can't relax*. How will anything get done? Some days I get so wound up over insignificant things and that's when the panic attacks start.

Abruptly, I am struck down by a sudden fear. I can't breathe. As I gasp, the fervent knot in my stomach begins to travel up towards my throat. Shaking convulsively, I try to grasp at my senses as the whole world spins like a merry go round. My heart is pounding in my chest. The blood is booming in my ears. Wide and wild, I must look like a madwoman: hot, flustered, embarrassed and with loose loops of hair clinging violently to my forehead. I wring my hands and try to push the tight ball of terror back down into its hiding place in the pit of my belly. I know I am being irrational but I just can't...just can't ...can't...can't...stop the overflow of suppressed tension.

I'm hardly in the mood for being sociable today. I am positive that horns must have sprouted from my head during the night. I couldn't sleep last night and now my whole fucking day has gone wrong since the moment I opened my sticky eyes:

Insomnia

Head rolling on the pillow,
Eyes rolling towards the window;
Luminous eyes, immense like saucers.
The midnight blue sky is sound
And lullabye trees are shushing in the wind.

Next door,
The TV volume is turned down low
But the voices are rolling,
Vibrating across the floor boards,
Rocking the bed.

Tossing,
My head feels emptier than the moon,
I roll over,
Locking my quilt in a steep embrace
And I breath deeply into darkness.

Wake up, still tired. Disorientated, I slip on a brown black banana that I forgot to eat x days ago. As I slip downstairs to deposit the inedible squidgy thing in the bin, I meet my father in the kitchen and he announces: 'I was watching Bruce Lee this morning.' He is referring to the kung fu video that Brian lent me.

'Oh really,' I snap, 'Did you remember to rewind it back to the part that I was watching?'

'I rewound it to the start,' he replied, smiling, obviously thinking he had done me a favour.

'What did you do that for?' I start screeching like a banshee on high speed dubbing and gesticulating, wildly. 'I had it set up at a specific point. I–I–I–HATE YOU.'

As soon as my temper tapered, I was going to insist that he manually find the place on the video again but he had already left for work.

Now, I'll have to do it myself.

I didn't care that my dad would've been late for work if he'd stopped. I only recognized the fact that there was a blip in my morning routine. It didn't matter that I didn't have time to watch a kung fu film or that I was already behind schedule because of my temper tantrum –

Humph, why me? How do things always happen to me?

I'm chugging all the way to rehab on a falling-apart bus that smells like smoked salmon when I am suddenly inspired to check my electronic diary.

OH BLOODY HELL!

It's 7th March. How did it get to this time? I've lost a whole week. I thought this was last week. EVERYTHING IS RUINED. My dates are all completely FUCKED.

I need to use my stupid mobile. I NEED TO PHONE MY MUM.

'He-loo!'

'Hello, where are you, Lynsey?'

'On a bus,' I snap, impatiently.

'There's a lot of noise,' observes my mother.

'Well duh, it's a bus,' I reply, sarcastically.

'What is it, Lynsey?'

'I've just checked my diary and I can't go to the hospital on Tuesday.'

'Oh,' she pauses, 'Why not?'

'I'm doing that thing,' I expect her to look into my mind and immediately know what I am talking about.

'What thing?'

'That thing I'm doing!' I'm losing sense of the conversation and I can't remember why I phoned.

'How did you manage to forget?'

'Don't know. I thought it was the following week.'

'Did you not write it in your diary?' In Lynsey-language this translates as 'You are stupid, imagine forgetting something like that.'

'Yes!' I shriek, banshee-style.

People on the bus are turning round and looking at me and shaking their heads like those nodding dogs you see in cars.

Fuck off, nosey people.

'I've lost a whole week,' I panic, 'I thought it was last week.'

I can feel the knot in my stomach twisting and turning like tangled laundry inside a washing machine.

'OK, calm down. We can phone the hospital tomorrow. It'll be fine.'

'Right,' I replied, huffily.

Why couldn't I have thought of that?

There were all kinds of mad memory aids and techniques that clients at rehab used. And then there were all the different procedures we had to follow.

Colour coded, enlarged, <u>underlined</u>, highlighted,

categorized

and alphabetized to strengthen the visual memory.

It should've been drilled into my head that the first thing I had to do every morning was 'sign in', but I constantly forgot to sign the attendance sheets and I was often still in the building when I had apparently left.

There's this thing called the 'morning meeting'. It's just like being back in the adolescent unit and going to 'community meeting' except this only happens once a day at ten o'clock in the morning. Someone plays the chairperson and someone plays the secretary and the chairperson reads out what happened yesterday and the secretary writes down in the diary what happens that day.

That's a bit stupid I think because we've only just arrived so nothing's happened yet.

`Monday 23 March`

`WM is off sick. Lunch will be half an hour late today.`
`LC has a doctor's appointment this afternoon.`

There's this woman in rehab who always writes things down. She doesn't come to the morning meetings. She doesn't come in the mornings. I don't know her name; I just call her the secretary because she always transcribes every conversation she has into her notepad.

DAY 1

'Hello, what's your name?'
   'Lynsey.'
She scribbles it down in her notebook.

DAY 2

'Umm, what's your name again?'
   'Lynsey.'
   She writes it down again.

DAY 22

'Hello, what's your name? I don't think we've met.'

Yes, we have. You ask me this every time I see you.

'Lynsey.'

DAY 55,000

'Umm, what's your name again?'
   I grit my teeth and smile.
   'Lynsey.'
   'And why is it you're here?'
   'I had a head injury.'
   'Yes, but why are you here?'

The same as you, you dosey cow.

'To get rehabilitation.'
   'Why don't you just get a job?'

Why don't you?

My tolerance level was stretched to the limit with her. If she wasn't telling me to go out and get a job, she was telling me to write in my diary.

If I spent as much time as she does writing everything down, I'd never do anything. It's not as if it even does her any good because she forgets to read it afterwards.

My mum got me an electronic organizer. I didn't like the instructions because they had all these arrows and lines pointing to buttons so I just flung them away in the bin with the guarantee. It was a good organizer when I finally worked out how it worked. I could put up to thirty names and addresses and phone numbers in one memory bank and in the other I could log in all the films I wanted to watch on television.

'That's not what it's for,' said my sister.

'I give up,' said my mum.

'Well, it's not my fault there's no room to put in hospital appointments.'

'You don't even watch all those films,' said my dad.

'You can tape them.'

'You don't even watch them when I do tape them.'

'Well, I don't like watching the telly, it gives me a sore head.'

When I exhausted all the possibilities of the little organizer, my mum and dad got me a palm top. It was shiny silver with a flip up screen and a special pen called a stylo. There was a little keyboard at the bottom of the screen and you just tapped it with the pen and you could write whatever you wanted.

'You'll have to be really careful with it, Lynsey,' my mum said, 'it cost a lot of money.'

'Yeah, yeah, yeah.'

'Do you want us to buy you a special case for it.'

'No cause that means I have to take it out my bag then take it out a case and blah de blah, that's a lot of hassle.'

Leaving to go to rehab

'Where's my ba—

CRASH

183

I find my bag all packed and ready.

On the way to rehab

SMACK.

I whack my bag off a metal thing on the bus.

Good, my sandwiches aren't squashed.

Inside rehab

SMACK-**BANG**-WALLOP.

'Whose bag is this?'
One of the clients is holding up my Winnie the Pooh bag.
'You'd better not have squashed my sandwiches!'

On leaving rehab via the stairs

'Do you want to see my new organizer?' I slap my bag down onto the table, stick my hand in without looking and rummage around till I feel the cold of the metal. 'Oops.'

Bump.

Bump.

Bumpitty-bump.

I chase my diary down the stairs.

The next day at the hospital.

'Show off your new diary,' says my mum.
'Ok,' I smile, unwittingly, and draw the new toy from my bag.
'Lynsey,' gasps my mum, 'it's all scratched.'

'Oh, how did that happen?'

Brian is always leaving his memory at home. He's got the same kind of pocket organizer that I used to have. Rehab thought that Brian was a bad influence on me because of his:

- poor attendance

- poor time-keeping,

which were a result of his

- all-night parties

- alcohol binges,

which manifested into his

- all-day hangovers.

Huh, I'm a good influence on Brian: he wants to come to rehab now so he can go for a drink with me afterwards.

I THINK I AM SLIGHTLY DRRUNK. IT WAS NOT MY INTENTION BUT AFTER TWO MEASLY BOTTLES OF HOOCH SUDDENLY THE WORLD SEEMS LIKE A NICER PLACE. IT IS SOMETHING THAT HAPPENS TO MOST PEOPLE AFTER A HEAD INJURY. THE DRINK, IT EITHER SUCKS YOU INTO AN ALCOHOLIC CHASM OR IT JUST PLAIN PISSES YOU OFF BY FLOORING YOU IN THE YOUTH OF THE NIGHT. APPAR

I've lost the plot, the place – I can't remember what I was saying. I am scribbling away on a piece of paper and I bet it was an important piece of paper but, just now, I don't give a fuck cause I'm happy and relaxed and happy and IT'S JUST BECOME APPARENT THAT I'VE WRITTEN A WHOLE PARAGRAPH IN CAPITALS.

I got a text message from Brian:

13 April 19:24

I jus8my1st subway and it was cool.

Brian

Eh?

'Hello'

'Hey Brian!'

'Hey Lynsey! Did you get my text message?'

'Yeah, I just got in. What are you doing tonight?'

'Oh, couple of my mates are coming over.'

'Imagine getting drunk with two bottles of beer.' I guffaw loudly down the phone.

'I think that's a case of the kettle calling the kettle black.'

'Eh?'

'Or is it the kettle calling the pot black?'

'Eh?'

'Never mind.'

'What are you doing?'

'I just got something to eat in Subway.'

'Right, what are you doing tonight?'

'Oh, just having some people over at the flat.'

'Did you have a nice time today?'

'Yeah. It was cool.'

'What are you doing tonight?'

'For the third time, I am having some people over.'

'Eh?'

'That's my mates, I need to go.'

'Eh? Right, I'll see you later.'

Apparently, head injury does that to you. It heightens the affect of alcohol. Apparently, one drink consumed by a head injured person is equivalent to three drinks to a 'normal' person. I hardly ever drink nowadays so this warm floaty feeling is rather novel.

We were too creative for rehab. I wanted to write poetry and plays; act, work in the theatre. Brian wanted to take photographs, make videos, paint pictures.

A typical outing to the job centre

'Fancy working as a toilet attendant?'

'No, but perhaps you'd like to be a floor technician.'

'Why don't you apply for this;' said Brian, with mock sincerity, 'Working in an abattoir.'

One of our projects was to research a job that we would like to do.

'Later,' said the job coach, 'you will be called in on mock interviews.'

We were given a list of jobs that previous clients had gone on to: sales assistant, receptionist, bank clerk, bookkeeper, office administrator...

BORING BORING BORING!

'I don't want to do any of these jobs.'

'Well, Lynsey,' sighed the job coach, 'what do you want to do?'

I took a deep breath and opened the yellow pages.

I will find a job.

I phoned every available community arts group:

'No.'

'I'm sorry we can't help.'

'We're far too busy.'

Until...

'I'm sorry we can't help you...'

'Oh.'

'Wait, why don't you phone this number...'

'Thanks.'

'They work specifically with actors who have disabilities.'
So I did.

Outreach and development workshops? Training possibilities?

'Our aim is to provide professional opportunities for people with disabilities.'

Wow!

'Actually, we're about to start a series of writing workshops. Would you like to come along?'

Chapter 12

Work

Today's Monday. I'm bored. It's the middle of June but it's cold and it's raining outside and the thought of going to work tomorrow depresses me.

Work. Huh. It's not even a real job. Everyone else has their own house and their own car and a job. When is it going to be me? No one else lives with their parents .

Ever since I turned sixteen, I've envied the rest of my friends who I'd watch going out after school to their part-time jobs in the chip shop or corner café.
'I want a job. Everyone else has a job.'
'But you've got your paper round.'
'No, that's not a real job. All my friends have got part time jobs, working in shops.'

SILVER SERVICE WAITERS/
WAITRESSES WANTED

I got an application form. A big mad seven-pager of an application form with loads of big mad weird humungous questions.
'Mum, do I have a National Insurance number?'

The mothe. bought me a long black pinafore for the interview and new black slip-on Kickers shoes; I wore one of my white chino school shirts.

'I'm not having you go out like a tramp.'

Oh good, I can wear this to school, tomorrow.

I knew a few people from school, who were going for the interview too: we all got the job. I was surprised when the mushroom-headed interviewer only spoke to us individually for about five minutes, barely skimming over our relevant details before sending us for the practical interview.

There was a long white table with about ten chairs ganging up on it and another table with all shiny silvery knives and forks and cutlery and fancy drink glasses. The fat glass was for red wine, the skinny glass for white.

Or was that the opposite way about?

There were teaspoons and soup spoons and sugar bowl spoons; meat knives and fish knives; meat forks and cake forks; loads of different cutlery and we had to remember them all.

There was a special way to hold the plates on your wrist and on your hand at the same time; there was a certain side you had to stand when you were serving people; there was a certain way you had to hold the meat and the vegetable between a fork and a spoon and you were only allowed to serve with your left hand.

There was a proper way to do everything but I managed to get it wrong every time: I speared the meat and potatoes; dropped the forks in the gravy; burnt myself on the hot plate; but I did get some of the left-over after-dinner mints to take home and the chef gave me a plate of ice cream because he liked me.

I was buddied up with real laugh-a-minute to help serve at her table. 'Trust me to get a vegetarian and a trainee on the same night,' she moaned. She sent me back to the kitchen for the back-up veggie meal and on the way back I got lost.

In and out those dusty bluebells...

In and out the function suites, through the restaurant and back to where I started in the kitchen. I got side tracked talking to the nice-looking dishwasher guy who smacked my bum with a dish towel when I turned round.

'What kept you?'

'Oh, I got lost.'

SIGH.

'Right take this tray of vegetables over to table six.'

'I thought we were table four?'

'Well, we're table six now because the other trainee needs a hand.'

The buddy looked at me, shaking her head. I tried to lift the hot tray—

OH!

'Use your towel,' she hissed, in an exasperated voice.

It was heavy and hot and burning me through the towel; sliding off my arm.

'Other arm. You're supposed to lift it with your right arm.'

I'd just die if I dropped it on someone's lap .

I'd listened to all the stories about people being scalded with soup and I was sure that was going to be me. I stuck the job for six whole weeks and I didn't scald anyone, but I did splash some gravy on the tablecloth when I was dishing out the meat. 'Oh, sorry.'

SIGH.

I dropped the bread and butter fingers face down on the kitchen floor. 'Oh, sorry.'

SIGH.

The glass of wine just slipped out of my hand. 'Oh, sorry.'

SIGH.

'Oh, sorry – How many people did you say wanted melon starters?'

SIGH.

'Oh, sorry – Did you say four melon starters and six prawn cocktail?'

SIGH.

'Oh, sorry– I thought you said four prawn cocktails?

SIGH.

'Oh, sorry. I'll have to hand in my notice. I've got so much work for school…'

'That's fine.'

CLICK. The phone went down .

They must have been glad to see the back of me. I hated that job. I didn't want to tell the mother after all the fuss that I made. I was so glad when she said to me, 'Lynsey, maybe this job isn't such a good idea with your prelims coming up…'

'I know, I'll have to concentrate on my exams, lots of work, what a shame…mmm…such a shame…'

Brilliant. No more burnt fingers. And no more moany waiter people.

Four years later, when college stopped for the summer holidays, rehab found me a work placement in a Glasgow bookshop. I was treated like any other employee except my hours were fixed, 1 a.m. – 3.p.m. every Tuesday and Thursday (unlike everyone else's infuriating ever-changing shifts) and, oh, I didn't get paid.

The job coach from rehab came with me on the first day. I was paranoid that people would find out that I was not a 'normal' worker like everyone else.

I hope they don't find out I go to rehab because I can't be bothered explaining that I'm not a drug addict.

Thankfully, I started on the same day as three other new trainees and we all took part in a week's training course as booksellers. One of the trainees, Linsay, was the same age as me; she had long brown hair and blue eyes just like me and she had gone to the same college. The other two trainees were both called Simon, both twenty one and both at Strathclyde University. We were introduced collectively as: 'Lynsey–Linsay– Simon–Simon'.

On the first morning, we were ushered into a boring I-need-a-black-coffee-to-wake-me-up staff meeting. Blah blah, blah blah blah.

Who wants to know how many gardening books we sold last month and I've never seen a real £50 note never mind a fake one and I need the toilet so I wish he'd hurry up and stop talking.

The most interesting thing, I thought, was when we were told to look out for a girl who'd been signing cheques under the name of Zoë Smith. Apparently she'd taken out the entire first series of *Friends* and then brought the videos back and exchanged them for series two *then* brought those videos back and exchanged them for series three.

Wow, series four isn't even out yet, I wonder what she'll get instead?

The section I was allocated was the poetry section. I enjoy alphabetizing, filing and 'flushing' (straightening up) the books, neatly on the shelves.

I don't have to talk to any annoying customers, except the ones who like reading poetry.

I liked talking about poetry and I even convinced several people to buy Sylvia Plath's *The Bell Jar*. 'This is an excellent book. It's very popular,' and 'Oh, if your daughter's studying Sylvia Plath, you should buy *The Bell Jar*.

Hmm, I need to read this 'Bell Jar' book. Everyone seems to be buying it.

I also put up posters with slogans on them on the backs of the book-cases.

'Ted's new poetry book would make an excellent birthday present'

'The sales in the poetry department have gone up thirty per cent,' announced the chairperson at the next staff meeting. Ted Hughes' *Birthday Letters* has sold fifty-five copies already.'

I think I might buy that book. I get a staff discount.

However, while I excelled in my own space, I couldn't seem to grasp any of the other duties expected of me.

The Main Information Desk:

Brrriiinngg brrriiinngg…

I reach over to answer the yelping phone just as an anxious, practically cross-legged creature starts flapping towards me.

Shit, who do I talk to – the phone or the person?

Brrriiinngg brrriiinngg
Another phone begins to ring.

Brrr-brrrriiinngg-iinngg-iinngg

'Can you tell me where the toilets are?'
  Brrriiinngg brrriiinngg

Shut up, stupid phone!

'Umm, the toilets are downstairs in the basement.'
  'Thanks. Where's the basement?'

???

When I was finally free to answer the phone, I
  Brrriiinnnggg
  'Hello, how can I…'
  CLICK.
  Brrriiinnnggg
  'Hell–'
  CLICK.
  'Lynsey, you have to press that button before you lift the receiver.'
  Brrriiinnnggg
  'Hello, how can I help you?'
  'Uh-huh, and who was the author?'
  Tap-tap, tap tap tap.
  'Who did you say wrote the book, again?' I'd have to ask the same question about a million times before I finally made sense of what I was actually being asked to look for. 'Ok, we should have a copy of that book in the store, I'll just put you on hold while I check.'

This is the bit that I hated the most: running up and downstairs like a headless chicken, around eight different floors before I finally located the section I was looking for (then half the time the book would be up in the stock room).

Meanwhile, I'd leave some poor fool dangling on the end of a miscellaneous telephone line. Later, I'd return, either having been sidetracked by some other customer or

Could Lynsey C call 221, could Lynsey C call 221

That pager-thing sounds like the guy from the *The Wizard of Oz*: 'I am Oz, the great and powerful. Who are you? I repeat, who are you?'

Could Lynsey C please call 221, Lynsey C call 221

Oh, that's me! Who wants me now?

And later, if I ever did remember to phone the customer back, I'd just plain forget what phone I'd left them hanging from.

And then there were the till points.

I hate the bleeping tills.

BLEEP
   'Press this for cash sales.'
   BLEEP
   'Press that for cash refunds.'
   BLEEP
   'Swipe credit cards like this.'
   BLEEP
   'You have to fill out a white form.'
   'No, it's the pink form.'
   'What are you doing? You're supposed to use the yellow form!'
   'Here's what you do with the book tokens.'
   'This is what happens with shipping orders...'
   'You'll never get a shipping order, we hardly ever get shipping orders.'

Second morning on the job after the training was finished, guess who got a shipping order... I called a line manager and he explained the process, again.

Second afternoon on the job, guess who got a shipping order... I called a line manager to explain the procedure again.

This is too complicated. Hope to god I don't get another one tomorrow.

The best part about working in the bookshop (aside from the discounts) was that I got to watch all the silly shoplifters through the nosey cameras.

I'd make a great store detective.

'Look at him trying to put that big Celtic bible in his bag,' I nodded to the security guard.

'Go on, take it,' said the security guard, 'I'm watching you.'

'Look at him,' I commentated, 'He's taking the biggest book on the shelf.'

What an idiot, does he think he's invisible?

'Oh there he goes, gotcha!'

As time went on, I was expected to work faster.

fasterfasterfasterfasterfaster

Tap-tap-tap...
Briiinggg...

Could Lynsey C call 222

'Hello could you...'
'Would you...'

'Where do I…'

'How much…'

The shop was getting busier, there were more customers to serve, more refunds to give, more fake money to watch out for and not enough time to watch the entertainment on the CCTV anymore.

My placement had been extended from six weeks to three months. Rehab and the bookshop were pleased with my progress. So pleased that they offered me a permanent position.

Heebie jeebies man, you must be joking! I'd go nuts in here. There's too many things to remember.

I was having panic attacks, dropping money, jamming my fingers in the tills and cutting people off the phone on a half-hourly basis. I'd had enough. 'Thanks for the offer but I think I'm going to go back to college.'

Chapter 13

Inspiration + the Road Ahead

Neilston
Ardrossan Harbour
Poole
Newton
East Kilbride

I scrutinise the neon writing on the black board: time, platform, destination; still no sign of the Ayr or Largs train.

I've been waiting for aaaages.

Impatiently, I hop from one foot to the other, panicking that the platform number will never roll up.

He's coming off the Ayr or the Largs train. Don't know which one.

DUUURRRRRRRRUUUUUUUUUUUHHHHHHHHHHHHHHH

Trains plough past on either side of me.
I scan the station clock.

Five past one. Maybe he's here already? I'm late. I'm late but I'm not late.

I run round in circles, past a man driving a big truck thing; two men in neon waistcoats and helmets like something from *The Empire Strikes Back*, storming through the place with their brown canvas sacks, lumpy with coins; a group of school kids in brown blazers, polished shoes and tidy rucksacks; goths in Green Day t-shirts, chains on their washed out denims, silver jewellery and other miscellaneous body piercings.

I fly past a row of silver phone boxes and WH Smith; heading straight towards the big white i of the information point. There are big white squares with numbers on them hanging from silver strings on the ceiling:

11

That must mean platform 11.

There's platform 11 on my left; platform 12 and 13 on my right and a big clear glass booth smack in the middle that says *'Virgin trains customer lounge.'*

The information point is a useless, big, white windmill-shaped stand, with blue posters advertising short breaks on Scotrail.

Prices From £89

Cheap Trips for the Over 60s

Family Funday Sunday

Midweek Mover

Information my arse, I need a map to find my way about!

I walk towards platform 12 and the chocolate machine, next to the free *Metro* newspaper stand.

I think he said it was platform 12 or platform 13

or

it could have been platform 11 or platform 10.

There are no *Metros* left, there never are. The woman that gives out the *Metros*, she used to always get me in the morning. I used to get lynched half a dozen times a day, walking past the station. Now there are never any *Metros*.

```
I watch a hackney scooting round the bendy road bit with
                                                         the
                                  criss-cross
                 yellow lines.
```

There's a mountain bike and two racers chained up at the green rails where the cars go past, a sign that says 'Caution Vehicles' and a yellow triangle with an exclamation mark inside it.

Round about to platform 10, round the other side of the Virgin Customer Lounge and the sign that says 'left luggage' ...*I left my luggage in the left luggage office...*

Singing Kettles, where did that come from?

DUUURRRRRRRRUUUUUUUUUUUHHHHHHHHHHHHHH

Platform 9.
Platform 8.
     13, 12, 11, 10, 9, 8...

DUUURRRRRRRRRUUUUUUUUUUUHHHHHHHHHHHHHHHH

I still can't find him.

DAH-DOO-DOOOOO

What was that?

'...train coming from _____ has been cancelled...'

Oh what? I missed that!

I spy a big, white plastic, cubic map, hanging about six foot above my head with all the little squiggles of information: There's arrows chasing each other, climbing up the way:

↑   Gordon Street

⇑   Queen Street Station

↕   Station manager

↕   Lost property

♂   Gents

♀   Ladies

How are you supposed get there? – Climb through the roof?!?

DAH-DOO-DOOOO

'The 12:55 train coming from Ayr will be arriving shortly at platform 12. Sorry for any inconvenience.'

That's it! It's got to be.

I run through the station: The Sock Shop, Whittards, Claire's Accessories, toilets; I'm hurrying, hurrying, hurrying.

The train station people won't let me past the chocolate machine. They've put a barrier on the platform.

I've got to get past.

'I've got to get past!'

'Can I see your ticket?'

'Not got a ticket.'

Blah blah blah. It takes an age to explain to them why I *need* to get on that platform. Finally, they agree to put an announcement over the big speaker things.

Here he comes, thank god for that!

'Here he is,' said the ticket collector guy, turning to Michael, 'she thought she'd lost you!'

Humph.

'Hi, Lynsey!' Michael waves to where I'm not standing.

'Hi, Michael!'

'Trains are dodgy.'

'I know.'

'What platform is this?'

'Platform 12.'

'Platform 12 ?!?'

'Yeah, you'll never believe what just happened…'

'…Do you want to see my new cane?' He takes a tiny white metal pole from his pockets, unfolds it, hands it to me; it's cold and skinny with a rounded stump on the bottom

WHEEEEEEEEEEEEEEEEEEEEE

that rolls when I wheel it along the smooth floor.

'You can take my arm.' I lightly touch his right lower arm with the back of my left hand.

I met Michael at the theatre group for people with disabilities; the first thing I clocked was his crazy white boots: Kickers; the next week, it was the blue Kickers, then the grey Kickers.

'Cement coloured,' he corrected, 'I've got a pair of green suede ones as well, but they're too small for me.'

'I've got a pair of stone Kickers shoes; I used to have a pair of black Kickers; I've got a Kickers bag and a Kickers jumper.'

When I went home to tell my mum that I wanted a pair of white Kickers boots she said, 'Oh, you used to have blue Kickers when you were younger.'

'Boots or shoes?'

'Boots and shoes. You were the first person at primary school to get Kickers.'

To the very first email Michael sent me, he attached a song from Disney's Alice In Wonderland:

How did he know? I didn't even say I liked *Alice in Wonderland*. Did I?

'No, you didn't tell me. I love *Alice in Wonderland*. I just bought the Disney film for my four-year-old niece.'

It was just one of those weird synchronicities. I had met someone who was as mad as a hatter.

Another Alice fan, but he's never read the book.

So we emailed back and forth for a couple of months; met up once a week with the rest of the group, and when the drama workshops ended, we arranged to go out for lunch.

There are hundreds and thousands of people sprinkled around the taxi rank, outside the station. I wave my eyes from left to right then back again.

'Hang on, I think we've come out the wrong exit.'

'No, it's fine. See, if you just turn to your right...'

My eyes swivel to the right.

'Can you see a set of traffic lights?'

Right, right, right, my eyes glaze over the traffic lights; pause, swing back to the traffic lights. 'Yeah.'

'It's just across the road.'

We slowly move towards the traffic lights, my arm linking Michael's. I poke the white inverted button; watch the red man morph to green; notice there's no beep-beep-beeping to indicate it's time to cross; it suddenly dawns on me, how selfish I have been, all those times I've moaned about the noise and mimicked the silly voices of the traffic lights near my house that stuttered: 'Traf-fic. Go-ing. To-the-town-hall. Has-been. Sig-nalled. To-stop.'

There are bumps in pavement like little round nipples, to help blind people across the road. A blind man walks in step with us, led by a luminous yellow-coated Labrador.

'Can you see Woolworth's?'

I clock the big red and white Woolies sign.

This is where I get my bus – just down here.

'I know where we are!'

We keep walking along Argyle Street, arm in arm.

'You're a good guide.'

I smile to myself.

That's because I've read the *Sighted Guidelines* on the net:

NOTE: Walk at a pace that is comfort-able for both people. The guide should not be 'dragging or towing' the follower and the follower should not be pushing the guide.

I always like to be aware of others' disabilities, so that I can make adjustments if there are ways I can accommodate them better: like at rehab, where that guy who could speak sign language taught me how to introduce myself, just in case I ever met anyone with a hearing impairment.

> Hello [wave left], my [fist clenched to chest] name [salute with two fingers] is Lynsey [finger spell]. Today [palms upwards, moving in], I would [folded index finger to cheek] like [hand on heart] to talk [pointing index fingers, on top of each other] about [point finger on palm, clockwise] British [point finger up, palm down, circling above] Sign Language [rub two palms together, take one away]. Many [wave fingers, pull outwards] deaf [two fingers, tap ears] people [touch cheek, mime beard] use [two fingers and thumb, pinch other thumb] British sign language to communicate [two 'c' shapes]. Hand shapes [mime Rubik's cube], facial expressions [circle face], lip reading [circle lips with index finger] and finger spelling [finger tips touching, wiggle] play an important [middle finger, touch palm] part in communicating with deaf community [make donut shape].

And I've taught Michael how to sign, 'Hello, my name is Michael,' just in case he ever meets a deaf person.

> Why [point to opposite shoulder] not [two pointing fingers [abrupt], slicing downwards]] try [two pointing fingers rub against each other] your [point] name?

'What's the street you're looking for again?'
   'Don't know, it's next to C&A.'
   'Cross the road as if you are going in to Woolworth's, then turn left and keep walking until...'
   'It's ok,' I hop up and down, 'I know where we are!'

Inside the vegan café, we have to waltz around a disarrangement of chairs.

'Do you want to sit here?' I line Michael up with the chair, take his hand and run it down the wooden back and then across the bum of the seat.

'You'll need to pull the chair out a bit.'

GUIDE: Position the follower in, so that the follower's knees touch the front of the chair. For some followers it may be helpful to describe the back and arms of the chair.

FOLLOWER: Bend to the chair, sweep the seat with one hand, locate the arms and sit.

'I've never been in a vegetarian café.'

Vegan.

'Do you want me to read the menu?'

'Yes, please.'

'...pitta bread with mushroom or aubergine pate, hummus...'

'What's hyoomiss?'

'Oh, it's really nice, it's umm...it's really nice.'

A café staff woman approaches our table several times before we finally order. I feel really guilty because I have to interrupt what Michael is saying, as she sneaks up on us with her little blank note book and pencil for the umpteenth time.

'Excuse me a minute, Michael – do you want an Irn Bru?'

I hope he doesn't think I'm being patronising. I know he likes Irn Bru and it's just easier than going through the entire drinks menu.

'I'll have a sparkling mineral water and could I have the hummus and pitta bread.'

She's looking at Michael and he's just sitting smiling away.

SILENCE.

'What was it you wanted, Michael?'

'Pasta.'

Now, she's kind of clocked on that he can't read the menu and she's looking at me for help.

I can't remember what he wanted; there's six different pasta dishes.

'Was it the carbonara?'

'What kind of pasta is that?'

'It has a creamy cheese sauce and imitation bacon bits,' smiled the waitress, looking less uncomfortable.

'Sounds nice, I'll have that.'

When she walks away, he says, 'What kind of pasta is it?'

'It's nice, I've had it before.'

'No, is it pasta shells or twists or what?'

'Eh, don't know.'

When the plates arrive with Michael's steaming hot spaghetti, my chilled pitta pockets with a tri-colour salad, I watch Michael pat his hand round the surface area of his plate.

'Oh no, spaghetti.'

'Do you not like spaghetti?'

'It's fine, never mind.'

Every attempt at lassoing the spaghetti results in it falling through the teeth of the fork.

Even I can eat spaghetti without making a mess. Well, maybe not without getting red tramlines on my forehead.

Eventually, he gives up and sighs, 'I'll just have a cake!'

I want to show Michael where I used to work. He hasn't been in a bookshop for years.

'Well, it wasn't really work. I didn't get paid; it was through rehab.'

'Oh, I don't really go into many bookshops since I lost my sight.'

As we are walking past the Levi's shop, one of those annoying green bib people (the ones that collect for a different charity, every day of the week) hijacks us; I feel like I am not really here, like I am outside my body, watching the whole crazy scenario, like it's the other Lynsey who's making my lips move.

Charity Guy	Hi, spare a few seconds of your time… Oh hi! How's it going? Haven't seen you for a while?
Lynsey	Fine. Yeah. Fine. [*smiling*]
Charity Guy	Don't really see anyone from school, these days.
Lynsey	Yeah, I know.
Charity Guy	So what've you been up to? Still living in Renfrew?
Lynsey	Yeah. What about you? Still living in the same place?
Charity Guy	Yeah, still there. You at college now?
Lynsey	Yeah, listen I need to go.
Charity Guy	Yeah, tell your mum and dad I was asking for them!

ECU* of Charity Guy's badge, which says 'Craig'.

* Extreme Close Up.

Further down the road a bit, Michael says to me, totally innocently, 'Who was that then?'

Yeah, who was that?

'No idea. That happens to me all the time. Folk just come up to me in the street and I'm expected to know them.'
'Yeah, that must be really weird.'
'Do you think he really did know me or was just being nice?'
'Maybe just trying to get money.'
'His name was Craig.'
They're digging up Buchanan Street; we have to zigzag round holes in the pavements with grey and white pebbles spewing out of them; a blue van with a sticky out wing mirror.

S

M

A

C

K

I'm five foot three and could've walked right underneath it but he's at least six foot and I didn't even think about telling him to duck.
'Are you ok?'
'Oooh,' he said, rubbing his head, 'what was that?'
'A van mirror. Sorry I didn't think. Are you sure you're ok?'

We don't want you ending up at rehab as well.

I try to describe the bookshop and its eight floors: basement, lower basement, ground floor, first floor, upper first floor, second floor, upper second floor and staff room up the top.
'You need a map for this place,' said Michael.

'Actually, they do have maps.'

I want to look at the dream dictionaries in the body, mind and spirit section: 'I've had another dream about my teeth falling out!'

'Oh, I had a really weird dream the other night ...'

We were there for about two hours, with me dictating all the dream interpretations; then I finally suggested we take the books down into the very bottom floor where the café is.

It was quiet when we first arrived in the shop, but now there's a queue like a conga line.

'What would you like to drink?'

'Eh, what do they have?'

I look at Michael and then at the two-foot-high menus that are sprawled across the walls. '...latte, caf au lait, mocha, hot chocolate...'

'Can I just have an Irn Bru?'

```
                                  M
                               I
                            C
                         H
                       A
                     E
                   L
```

laughs; picks up the

glass to drink it and

nearly pokes his

right eye out but

hits his cheek

bone instead.

'Wow, there's a straw in this!'

Outside the bookshop, I start walking on automatic pilot, not really thinking what direction I'm heading:

'Oh, what direction did we come from?'

'I don't know.'

'I think it's up this way... No think it is up there.'

Round and round Buchanan Street and around the surrounding streets.

'What shops are on the right of us?'

'Going Places and a cocktail bar.'

'What about the left?'

'Thomas Cook and RS McColl .'

'Do you see George Square yet?'

'No.'

We come to a crossing in the road with lumpy pink pavements.

'What street is the book shop on?'

'Buchanan Street.'

'Buchanan Street ?!? – I thought it was up near Sauchiehall Street!'

'No, that's Waterstones. It's next to Pastimes.'

'Pastimes! I know where that is. Take me back to Pastimes, and we can get to the Central Station from there.'

Back to Pastimes, past Frasers, past the Levi's Shop and up Union Street until we get to the same crossing as we were at before.

'I don't believe it, if we had kept walking the first time we would have got to the station. We have walked round in a square!'

'I know the shops you were reading out to me earlier, that just proves that in order to know where to go, you need to know where you came from.'

Into the mouth of the station and up the escalator. It's nearly 8:00p.m.

'Do you know where the chocolate machine is?' asked Michael.

Chocolate machine? Chocolate machine?

'No.'

'O.k. Take me down to platform 12.'

I look up and around.

Platform 12, where are you?

The Sock Shop, Whittards, Claire's Accessories, toilets and finally, the chocolate machine. 'It might be a better idea to meet here the next time.'

We share the same train home. I'm sitting beside Michael showing off my mobile phone. Pointing at it and waving it about.

'You should really get one of these.'

'What's that, Lynsey?'

'You need to get one of these,' I bellow in his ear.

'Yeah,' he added, looking straight ahead, 'Do you fancy going to Partick, next week?' 'Absolutely!' I enthused, 'You be the memory and I'll be the eyes!'

From: 'Mikey H'
To : 'Lynsey C'
Subject: Yesterday
Date: Thurs, 10 May 2000 13:37:23 -0000

Hi Lynsey!

I hope you got home alright last night, my mum and dad met me at the station. That was one of the best days I have had in Glasgow and am glad we had a chance to talk rather than trail round the shops, which can get very tiring.

I had a dream inovling water

(Inovling? This is full of spelling mistakes)

again last night this time I went fishing in a river and caught a nice big rainbow trout it was very unusual.

Write soon

Michael

PS I have attached directions to the chocolate machine

DIRECTIONS TO CHOCOLATE MACHINE

EITHER FROM UNION STREET OR TAXI RANK ENTRANCE.

Walk towards the main digital display board with train times. Stand facing the board. Turn right and walk towards the shops like Our Price etc.

There isn't any Our Price in the station anymore.

Turn left at Our Price and walk forwards. Shops should always be on the right. Smaller digital display board should shortly be on the left, but keep to the shops on the right. The shops should finish and there is a big open space. You should see the stairs and escalators to the low level trains over slightly to the right. Walk towards the escalators. Once at the escalators, there is a wall to the left of them. At the edge of the wall, take a right towards the *Metro* paper stand, which is standing against the wall. The chocolate machine is just beside it.

FROM UNDERNEATH BRIDGE.

Walk past smelly chip shop.

(Oh yes, I know where that is.)

Keep walking until entrance to station on the right. Once inside, keep to the wall on the left. Go round the corner and keep to the wall on the left. Walk a few metres and cross over to the wall facing you.

Take a left and walk forwards, with the wall always being on the right. The escalators should be on the right. Once at the top of the escalators, take a right at the corner of the wall and walk about a metre towards the *Metro* paper stand which is standing against the wall. The chocolate machine is just next to it.

And we did meet at the chocolate machine the following week; we went to Partick, where I saw, and he smelled, a man smoking a hookah, in a Lebanese café; Irvine, Ayr, Arran, Edinburgh; we are talking about going on holiday next year, to Denmark.

☙

'Impenetrability, that's what I say'

(Meaning, according to Humpty Dumpty: 'We've had enough of that subject, and it would be just as well if you mention what you mean to do next, as I suppose you don't mean to stop here all the rest of your life'.)

Alice's Adventures in Wonderland, Chapter 6

I've come a   l   o   n   g   way.
A far cry from the time I couldn't even find the post box in my own street.

I hadn't been out of the house on my own since I left school. It was a struggle for my mother to even convince me to walk across to the post office with her. I stayed holed up in my bedroom most of the day, every day, writing poetry and kissing envelopes in the hope that this next poem would be the one that would be published.

'I've got another letter to post,' I whispered.

My mother was in the thick of a waist high pile of ironing.

SSSSSSSSSSSSSSSSSSSSSSSSSSSSSSSSSSSSSSSSSSSSSSSSSSSSSSSS

She didn't answer, just kept on pressing shirts, the steam of the iron hissing out through its impatient little nostrils.

'I need to post a letter,' I whined.

The iron exhaled an indignant little snuffle.

'Well, off you go,' she said, without looking up.

'What?'

'You know where the post box is.'

'Are you not coming?'

'Lynsey, I'm up to my eyeballs.'

'Oh, I need to post this.'

'Well, off you go.'

I thought about it for a moment. I'd been to the post box almost everyday this week with my mum.

I can do it.

I wasn't that sure, though.

'Mum, where is the post box, again?'

SSSSSSSSSSSSSSSSSSSSSSSSSSSSSSSSSSSSSSSSSSSSSSSSSSSSSSS

Letter in hand, I stalked the street, creeping along the concrete pavement. A row of grey obnoxious flats on my left and a steady stream of honky-tonk cars lined up outside the pub on my right. A chain of red, silver, yellow and white cars snaked along the black tongue of the road.

It was distracting, watching the little bugs on wheels out of the corner of my eye. I knew I had to focus on the pavement in front of me. 'Down the stairs and turn left and it's just straight ahead of you at the end of the road,' that's where my mum said the post box was.

Down the stairs and turn left and then straight ahead.

Down the stairs and turn left and then straight ahead

Down the stairs and turn head and then straight a left

Who put that pavement there?

Some one had stuck a baby road right in the middle of the pavement. I had to wait ten million seconds whilst two fat red cars squeezed their bums through the slender lane.

Turn the stairs and down left and head towards...I forget...

Up and down and to and fro and back and forth and up and down and to and fro and back and forth and up and down and to and fro and back and forth and up and fro and back and to and down and fro and back and forth and down and up and forth and down and down and up and fro and to and back.

Back back back home. It was getting dull. I climbed the stairs letter in hand.

'Lynsey, where have you been?'

HUH

'Posting a letter,' I huffed.

My mum looked at the scrunched up bundle in my hand and wrinkled her brow. 'You've been away for more than two hours.'

'Somebody,' I said, matter-of-factly, 'has moved it.'

'Moved what?'

'The post box.'

'No, it was there this morning. You cant just move a post box.'

'Well, it wasn't there. Someone's moved it. I've been up and down that road and it wasn't there,' I raged.

My mum put her jacket on and we marched back out of the house and down the miserable grey street.

'See that big red thing in the middle of the pavement, right in front of you,' she said, sarcastically. 'I told you no one had moved it.'

And sure enough, there it was: standing footless, trying to look innocent with its flushed red face and smarmy Cheshire cat grin, poking out at me, laughing at me from behind a wall of thin air.

I must have been walking right past it!

Finally I got to post my crinkled mail but I'd missed the last pick-up.

When I think about all the things I couldn't do and look at what I have achieved… A couple of years ago, I couldn't remember how to make a bowl of cereal without step-by-step instructions:

1. Take a bowl from the bottom left cupboard beside the cooker.

2. Take the cereal box from the far left bottom cupboard beside the fridge.

3. Open the box of cereal and pour some into the bowl.

4. Remember to leave space for milk.

5. Take the milk from the fridge and pour until cereal is partly covered.

6. Now get a spoon from cutlery drawer.

7. Be careful not to spill the milk.

8. Eat at the kitchen table.

My mother didn't go as far as to label the cupboards but I think if I was living alone then that's something I might have to think about. I can just imagine myself sticking post it notes all over the house and alphabetizing the groceries.

Living at home with your family means compromising and being aware of other people's needs. That means sometimes you have to take a step back and put the task that you are doing on hold.

I always hate it when I'm halfway out the door and my family launch into a big conversation:

'Oh, I nearly forgot to tell you…'

Or

'Wait a minute and I'll walk you down.' (And then ten million minutes later, I'm still waiting.)

Or

'You're not going out like that!'

Out like what?

'Fix that shirt! You've got the collar all tucked up like a dog's breakfast.'

And

'Tie those laces.'

And

'When are you going to get a haircut?'

Then it's

'Lynsey, you've left the grill on.'

And

'Lynsey, you've left the fridge door open.'

And anyway,

'What makes you think it was me that spilt the milk and dropped the cornflakes over the floor just because I had cornflakes doesn't mean to say and I never put the coffee in the fridge or my dirty washing in the bin and it wasn't my music you heard at six o'clock this morning didn't even have the computer on so how could I forget to disconnect it haven't even been on the net since it wasn't it wasn't it was not me I get the blame for everything in this house and now you've made me late and I've missed the bus and going to be late and you're always making me late and someone's stole my keys I've not got my keys what did you do with my keys I've got them in my pocket I'm going now.'

'Does someone want to walk me down to the bus stop?'

'I need to go to the bank who can remember my pin number I don't know my pin number you should know it I can't find my bank card that's my college card and that's my library card and that's last month's library card that I lost and the laminated one's my vegan society card and the cardboard card's for the flexible learning unit and that's my gym pass and that's my bus pass and how am I supposed to get money if I don't have a card?'

'Where are you going I thought you were walking me down I'm not ready yet I've still got to find my purse I can't go out without my purse and I've lost my gloves how's it my fault if folk steal my gloves no I'll not hurry up I'm reading I'm on the last chapter how'd you always have to spoil it when I'm in the middle.'

'Fine then I'll go myself you never do anything for me anyway never take me anywhere.'

'You need to give me money you told me to go to the supermarket myself how am I supposed to go when I don't have any money you never buy anything I like to eat I never said that I liked peanut butter I don't like potato scones that was last week and I don't have time to do the stupid ironing it takes ten million years and the jumpers won't even fold and I can't do shirts or pyjamas and how was I supposed to know that stretchy stuff doesn't iron well I was doing you a favour just wanted to surprise you you're always moaning saying I'm rubbish at everything and anyway I think the iron's broke cause there's no bit to put the water in.'

'When are you going to show me how to use the washing machine you keep saying you'll show me how to use the washing machine no I won't not if you show me then write down all the instructions why does that say *with prewash* I'm bored don't even know what all the buttons are for can I go now this is boring I'm meant to be going out.'

'When are you taking me away for the day you said you would take me away for a treat how can we not go somewhere I haven't been before I want to go to Dublin for the weekend see in the summer holidays can we go back to Isle of Man what time's the train I could go to the shops for a loaf for the sandwiches how's it always me that has to go to the shops I don't want to go to the shops I don't even want sandwiches how can we not just buy something when we get there?'

'Don't bug me I'm trying to read a book I can't read and listen his music's getting on my nerves this is boring are we nearly there I need the toilet I don't want to use that toilet it's smelly are we nearly there I need the toilet where's the toilet that toilet was humming that's your fault for making me drink gassy juice I want a drink I need the toilet are we nearly there yet where's the toilet?'

'What's this place called again can I go back to that shop I don't know I just wanted to buy something I don't know see you how am I supposed to remember everything how do we have to go into all your shops this is boring I want to go home what's that can we go in there that was good can we go to the Metro centre tomorrow?'

ZZZZZZZZZZZZZZZZZZZZZZZZZZZZZZZZZZZZZZZZZZZZZZZZZZZZZZZZZZ

Recently, I've begun to ask my mum what I was like as a child. With no memories beyond the age of fourteen and only fragments of my life over the last eight years, I wish I'd kept a diary. I say it all the time: 'I'm going to start writing a diary.'

I have a large red diary with 'a week to view' for everyday reminders such as going to the shops, taking books back to the library, and college homework.

I have a slim black diary for my writing, the poetry and prose I send, what magazines I submit to, what's been accepted for which publication, and what has been rejected.

I have a notice board made of cork on the back of my door (I don't like to put it above my bed in case it falls on my head and I end up like *Flat Stanley*) with bus and train timetables, schedules for the gym, swimming baths and college classes and a calendar for dates with friends.

I have a book of birthdays and a book of addresses. I keep telephone numbers listed on my mobile phone and email addresses in my Yahoo account address book. I plan to duplicate them all when I buy a new diary.

My friends at college thought I was well organized until last week when I misplaced my everyday diary. My family know better.

They are the ones who've had to phone round friends' houses, the college, the bus companies, when I have lost my diary, my gloves, my jacket, my shoes…

Reference

Carroll, L. (1865) *Alice's Adventures in Wonderland.* Middlesex: Puffin Books, 1962.